Dear Alisa ~

thank you for
everything you
have done for me

with love & respect

Robin

Secrets Hidden

By the Side of the Road

Robin Taylor

ISBN: 978-1-4624-0099-7 (e)
ISBN: 978-1-4624-0100-0 (sc)

Library of Congress Control Number: 2012935900

Inspiring Voices books may be ordered through booksellers or by contacting:

Inspiring Voices
1663 Liberty Drive
Bloomington, IN 47403
www.inspiringvoices.com
1-(866) 697-5313

Printed in the United States of America

Inspiring Voices rev. date: 5/10/2012

Contents

Acknowledgments

I would like to give special thanks to Mark Madama and Eric for saving my life. Also, to my Uncle Dick and Rusty for their heart felt support and bankroll.

To the Doctors who have kept me alive and stable, Dr. Herbert Fox, Dr. Ilisa Wallach and Dr. Ronald Hoffman and my life guides, Clancy Imislund and Kevin Heaney.

To all those wonderful friends and talents who took my 'scratching's' – Raymond, Rena, Amye, Gina and Lucy from 'Inspiring Voices' and put ink to my words.

Also, the friendships from Chris and Dick at POLICH/ TALLIX Foundry, New York City's FOUNTAIN HOUSE and GALLERY and Wayne Bryan from the MUSIC THEATRE OF WICHITA.

But, most of all to my husband Mark and our two cat's, Oscar and Jenny who must live with me everyday. I give deep thanks...

Dedication

"I dedicate this book to my older brother, Johnny, who watches over me from above..."

RT

Prologue

Missouri Nightmare

Summer 1956

A long stretch of Missouri road broke through the scorching vapors of a late afternoon haze. It was the end of summer, and the dusty tail of a dark green Mercury whipped along the hollow between lion-colored hills.

"We're taking you home now, Miss Jones," drawled a syrupy female voice with a thick Georgia accent. "Mister Jones is waiting for you."

"I'm not Miss Jones; I'm Robin Rae Schillereff," the child pleaded. "I'm your little girl. I'm Robin. Robin Rae Schillereff!" She started to cry. "I'm not a Miss Jones, I'm—"

Her older brother Johnny cut her off with loud yelps and dog barks. Then he shot his air rifle out the side window. The man driving joined in with the taunting. The three of them sang over the girl's persistent cries. This was a game that they played. The "where are you now, Little Miss Jones" game. Her parents had played it ever since she could remember.

Her mother saw something up ahead and tapped the sweating man on the shoulder. She pointed, and they both nodded in agreement. Her father took his foot off the pedal and slowed down the car. He pulled over to the side of the two-lane road, bringing the filthy Mercury to a stop.

When the dust settled, the woman opened the right front door and peeled herself from the seat. She was a slim, attractive woman, fine-boned with short, cropped hair tinted the color of tar. A Pall Mall dangled from her painted lips. She took one step back and opened the rear door, reached in, and lifted out her daughter. She placed Robin in the dirt about three feet from the car.

The little girl was dressed in a faded smock with just the hint of a white petticoat beneath it. Her straight vanilla hair had been cut into a china-bowl shape. She watched her mother walk between a broken cowboy fence and cornstalks. Turning around, her mother pointed to a desolate shack leaning on the rise of a hill.

"There's your home, Miss Jones. Mister Jones is waiting for you," she said. "Now go on."

The girl stood there, motionless.

"That's where you belong. You're not our little girl. We've just been keeping you till we found your husband, Mister Jones, and now we have, so go on." Then with a puff on her cigarette and a few hand flourishes she sashayed on back to the car. The car door slammed, and Robin heard low chuckles and hushed giggles.

The little girl tried to talk, but the words stuck in her throat. She was paralyzed and frozen with fear. The Mercury shuddered. Robin shook her head. *No, no!* The purring engine growled as the accelerator was pressed down. Her brother from his open window aimed the shiny long gun at her. Giving her a wide toothless grin, he cocked the air rifle and then fired. Bang! Immediately a large hand slapped him back into his seat.

"Go on in, now," her mother called out, tossing her cigarette butt into the dirt and pointing again toward the leaning shack. "Mister Jones has got supper on, and he's waiting for you to go on inside." Then with one last hand gesture she turned away.

The car rolled off the dirt and drove out onto the road. The girl disappeared momentarily under a cloak of swirling dust and fumes. When the cloud subsided, she saw that the car was driving away. Wiping the grit from her eyes she ran after the fading green car as fast as she could. After a few feet she tripped and sprawled flat, leaving her Buster Brown shoes behind in the dirt. She'd also lost her doll and crawled into the dry gully to look for it. Her tiny frame, rocking back and forth, convulsed with great sobs.

As the sun slowly set, she, walked toward the shack. Numb, she stared at the melting violet sky. The first twinkling of twilight hovered just above the grass. She listened to the whispering shadows and then, waiting, stood shoeless by the side of the road.

1

Dying Summer

Summer 1984

It was early August, close to midnight. The small maid's room where I had lived on and off for the past two years was immaculate. The wooden green cot was made up to look like a board. Every Hallmark collectible was displayed in its special place. Everything I owned was marked on the back or inside with a black Sharpie pen.

The black beauty capsules, white tablets, and red amphetamines were lined up on the worn beach mat like warring ants facing off. An open jug of Gallo stood among them like an imperious referee, the level of wine inside getting lower with every swig and swallow of a pill.

It had been a bad summer, and that night it felt worse. After fourteen years of marriage, Eric and I were calling it quits. He hated New York and had been living in Los Angeles ever since his theatrical bus and truck tour had ended over a year earlier. I hated Los Angeles, so our living situation was at a bicoastal standstill. Over the course of our long-distance calls and letters, I brought up divorce. The rock-bottom reason wasn't distance but rather the fact that Eric wanted children and I didn't. I was holding him back and knew in my gut that a divorce was the best thing for both of us.

Sitting on the table next to the wine bottle was a large manila envelope from the Superior Court of Los Angeles containing a petition for the "Dissolution of Marriage because of Irreconcilable Differences." The breakup had been a long time in coming, so the papers were no big surprise. Still, the sight of court's letterhead jolted me to the core.

I had been feeling a little low and physically sick for the past week, moody and teary-eyed for no reason I could name. I made sure that the light in my small bedroom was always on, that everything stayed in its exact place. I couldn't keep my room clean enough. If I slept at all, I had the sensation that I was drowning, sinking down through a bottomless lake in which I couldn't seem to find the surface. Comforting sleep was beyond my grasp.

Earlier that day, around three o'clock, I'd decided to get out of sweltering New York and visit Eric on the coast. Things were amicable between us, and I thought the change in scenery would do me good. I dragged myself down to Port Authority and took the bus to Newark Airport.

When I reached the USAir counter, I half-pushed/half-rolled my bag onto the luggage scale, told the woman my name, and handed her the slip of paper with my reservation number. Without looking up, she told me that the flight had been canceled. *Canceled? Why?*

She continued to explain and point to the board, but I couldn't hear her anymore. I wasn't absorbing her words. I felt like a sand castle after the first wave, dissolving into nothingness. I shuffled out of the terminal, feeling like I was nearing the final scene in the last act.

I don't remember how I got back to Manhattan. I stood on the northeast corner of Broadway and Eighty-seventh Street with my wallet wide open. Looking into the darkness between buildings, I saw moving shadows. I saw drug-dealing sentries all the way to my door. That was what I must do. I would take a cheap route to a quick end. After a short stop at the liquor store and a friendly wave at the doorman, I began a soft Burgundy roll into oblivion. *Eric, I gotta talk to Eric, just to say hi and hear his voice once more. He is—was—the best husband ever. That's right, I'm right, you're right, everybody's right. Right!*

I pushed my stiff back up against the building's water pipe and wall and forced myself to sit up straight, tall, and erect. Then, reaching under the mat, I jerked on the cord that led to the princess phone in my room. With two hard tugs it toppled off the second shelf and fell to the floor. Bam! Bam! The phone split in two. Strangely, I didn't hear it fall.

I sensed a flutter of activity around me—glints of flashing silver, distorted faces fading in and out. I seemed body-less. I was flying. It was only when I saw the doorman's ghoulish mask that it occurred to me that I must now be outside of the building. Someone lifted me up and slid me into an EMS vehicle. I must have struggled because I fell off the gurney. The bumpy, stainless-steel floor was the last thing I remembered—until I puked uncontrollably.

Vomit almost overflowed the edges of the kidney-shaped pan that had been stuck in front of my face. Between retches, I tried to raise my eyes to see who was holding the pan with this mess. My hands and arms dangled listlessly. After another attack, I managed to raise my head up expecting to see a nurse or doctor. But no—oh my God, it was Jack. *Not Jack.* Someone must have called him.

He was a reed player I knew from the road, an exceptional musician. We had been lovers on and off for the past year. Oh no, not Jack! I felt so humiliated. And then I had to puke again. Jack held me as I spewed my guts out all over his groin. I was totally mortified. Jack, with supreme dignity, took a towel and gently slid off the bed. He excused himself, parted the white curtain, and left.

I realized that I was now in what looked like a very busy emergency room. A nurse came over and closed the curtain, while another stepped through with a clean pan and checked my vital signs. Noise started to build as I became more conscious. How had Jack known that I was here? I should have been dead. Why wasn't I dead? What had happened? Who found me? I felt so awful.

I tried to get off the bed but stumbled. My legs felt like liquid. Someone in a white coat and with strong arms caught me, and I came face-to-stomach with a brilliant tropical garden with electric-blue parrots. *I'm really stoned*, I thought to myself. Before I could comprehend what was happening, another spasm overpowered me. I wiped my mouth with a clean towel, refocused, and looked up.

Thank God. What I'd thought was a trip to the World Wildlife astral plane was only a doctor's tie. After a bit of time and cleanup, people began to ask me questions.

The doctor was joined by a psychologist (perhaps she was a psychiatrist) and a male intern. The shrink asked all kinds of questions like, "Do you know your name?" and "Do you know where you are?". The two men left to deal with other patients, and then it was just me and the head doctor, who continued to grill me. She talked about the possibility of this being a suicide attempt and if I had intentionally overdosed. I managed from somewhere deep inside me to pull up a stable personal characterization of myself. I denied all her accusations that I was trying to commit suicide. I told her over and over that it was an accident, that I hadn't meant to overdose.

It finally worked. She signed a few forms, handed them to the nurse, and left. The doctor with the tie returned and said a few things to me. I smiled and nodded. Then he let in Mark, my tour buddy and good friend. The hospital was putting me into his custody. I was glad it wasn't Jack.

When Mark helped me down off the gurney, I realized how sore I was. It was like someone had used my stomach and ribs as a punching bag. Shoes—did I have shoes? I couldn't remember.

What was this? What the hell was I wearing? Oh, it was a hand-me-down denim jumpsuit that once belonged to my housemate, Sharon. Why this? It was three sizes too big, and worst of all, it was pink. I hated pink. I could feel it dragging around, hanging over my dirty penny loafers like a bad wig, but I was too exhausted to care. That Tony

Award–winning performance with the shrink had really taken its toll. It was about all I could do to follow Mark out of the hospital.

I stayed over at Mark's apartment. Curled up tight on the vinyl sofa, I stared vacantly into space. Later I watched the sun rise through the Ninth Avenue windows. I remember someone whispering conversations into the wall phone in the kitchen.

2

Pink Jumpsuit

Summer 1984

When morning finally broke, I was a different person. I was locked deep within myself under the many folds of denim. I felt like I was two inches tall, screaming to be heard, but no words came out. My legs were heavy. My mind was trapped behind a wall of paranoid, fathomless despair. I was in the throes of waking death. Whatever I had tried to run from had found me.

It was too bright; the glare was overwhelming, as was the noise. Sinking down into the folds of fabric, I tried to understand and obey Mark's hand gestures. Then we were outside. Pointing south, he headed toward the theater district, but I was paralyzed in the spot where I stood. Consumed with paranoia and frozen by the rush of cars, honking horns, and the jumble of people coming and going, I was completely dazed and disoriented. Then I saw Mark's wonderfully worn and dirty sneakers, which comforted me for some reason. Gently, ever so calmly, he maneuvered my leaden legs around steaming potholes, and eventually we crossed Eighth Avenue.

Then it happened. I propelled myself up and out of my body. I went to that numbing place. It was a safe place where I couldn't feel the searing pain or the roadside abandonment of my childhood. I was weightless and free, high above all feeling or care.

Over the heads of the agitated crowds, I put my two-inch-tall self squarely atop one of Mark's sloping shoulders. There, firmly planted, I looked at myself lumbering along: a sad and empty face and the body of a bloated whale, dressed in a cotton-candy-colored jumpsuit, and taking up most of the broken sidewalk. I knew this person, but I couldn't feel her. Mark walked on and on. I had no sense of time, emotion, or distance. Then suddenly all light had gone, and I couldn't breathe. It was dark. I was in a marbled lobby, and Mark was guiding me toward some elevators. A swarm of suitcases emerged from the elevators, engulfing us.

We walked into another small lobby, and Mark talked to someone over a high counter. I circled the room. There were plants, huge trees, and many office windows. I was too pink. I needed to hide my embarrassment. There in the corner was a tall tree. The stabbing branches tried to keep me out, but I managed to get around behind them. But they found me—Mark and a small lady in a cherry-red suit. The leaves on the carpet gave me away. Mark pulled me out, and we followed the red suit.

We went to a different office. It was dark. We sat down. I tried to answer the woman's questions, but I couldn't get the words out. I stammered and stuttered;

the words got stuck in my throat and came out all wet. There were forms for me to fill out. Over there. Mark came with me. The pen wouldn't write my name. *I can't even write my name.* Mark took the pen. He asked me questions. Shaking and stuttering, I answered from somewhere inside.

What theaters had I worked in?

What shows had I done?

What unions did I belong to?

It was so hard to think. Where had I put the answers?

Mark talked to the lady in the red suit as I tried to understand the forms. The words blurred into tiny blue bulbs as I moved the pen. From behind me, someone took the papers away. Then I was back in a comfortable chair facing the lady. Heads nodded; words were spoken. The red suit said the Lexington School for the Deaf in Jackson Heights, Queens, could help me. She passed some papers to me, and we shook hands. Mark led me out past the trees and into the hallway. At the elevator he turned back toward me. My gaze shifted from his shoes to his face; he looked so tired.

Then we were outside again. The sun was blinding, and I couldn't see Mark. I was terrified. Somehow he led me across the river to another big building.

It was cool inside. There was a big green hall with an office on the right. Children of all sizes were talking with their fingers as were their teachers and parents. Some of them glanced over at the pink whale, pointed, commented using their hands and arms, and then continued on and out of sight. Mark took me to another room further down the hallway. Lined up against the wall outside the room were low plastic chairs in finger-paint colors of orange and yellow and strange cutout backs with short legs.

A voice from inside the room asked us to come in. She was older than the lady in the red suit and had a soft crown of curly white hair. Mark talked and passed my papers to her. She spoke. Their eyes turned toward me, and again I stammered answers from somewhere beyond my face. Her mouth started to twitch. She picked up the phone repeatedly. She asked me to wait outside. I went; Mark stayed.

Feeling invisible, I watched the children leave. Some ran and were silently scolded. Others had hands filled with wet paintings; they pulled them like kites so they would dry. Some were alone; a few walked with stooped grown-ups. Then they were all gone.

From the other direction, an old cleaning man dragged the trash across the hallway. I was consumed by a bottomless void of nothing but waiting and waiting.

Suddenly, from out of the stillness, Mark was near my shoulder. It was time to go back into the room. I rose slowly and followed him, lost in the emptiness. The white-haired lady said I needed help. She said that she had made a few calls and was waiting for some answers. We sat and stared.

The white-haired lady picked up the phone. She talked and listened and talked. Mark answered and looked over to where I was sitting. He turned back and spoke again. They had a bed. It was available. The white-haired lady recommended it. It was at the Payne Whitney, next to the New York Hospital in Manhattan on the East Side.

I had to see the doctors in emergency, she said, and added something about an interview. They could help. Go.

Mark thanked the lady. I think I did too.

Outside the brightness had gone. The street lamps and porch lights were buzzing. Trailing after Mark, I walked away from the school, dragging along bits and pieces of my mind.

After we left the Lexington School for the Deaf, we took a train back in the city. At the hospital, I found wheels whished passed me on both sides as I was guided up a short, gray ramp. I seemed to be walking the center line on a gurney highway. We passed through glass double-doors into the crowded hallway. I trudged behind Mark, following him into a large room characterized by frenzy and filled with pain. A scream stopped me. I looked up and surveyed the chamber. A bleeding man, thrashing, was manacled and dragged from the room. The heel marks of his struggle pushed a woman in front of me to start sobbing.

Mark led me to a long, white counter. A small woman with a white hat stood behind it. *This must be another hospital*, I thought. Mark talked, and then she talked and passed some papers over. He led me to a table with a low, green, metal chair. Mark said he would be right back. Before I could speak, he left. Shaking and crying, I tried to fill in the spaces on the forms, but again, the pen wouldn't write the words. Someone was whimpering behind me. *Too much hurt*, I thought. *I must go deep and let the walls close in.*

Suddenly, I was in a different room. It was very dim, with only one hanging light. A man with a bushy mustache was beside me. It was a gentle and soft voice. The lamp glared over me. An outline of a large woman emerged from the shadows. When she spoke, her words were cold and unfeeling. Her booming voice pierced the air as the interview began.

During the interrogation, I caught glimpses of her. She had strong thick calves above polished shoes, and an eel-like face with gaping, sharp teeth. The stocky woman barked questions at me like, "Do you drink? Do you use drugs? Do you inject heroin?" over and over, silly questions with obvious answers. The mustached man sat over to the side. He just watched and wrote, drew and stared.

Why is this shark nurse so mean? Where's Mark? I tried to answer the questions, but they got all twisted inside. It seemed that this was the time of nothingness, and then of sudden change.

Instantly the lights were turned on. Mark was there, sitting in a corner. The shark nurse looked much kinder now. There were no big fangs. I caught her smiling at me. She and the mustached man talked to Mark, and then they left. Mark talked at me too. I wished he had made sense. I tried to keep my mind going. The people returned, and they chatted with Mark. He said something to me. He waved, and then he left. I was drained, empty. The woman was motherly then, and she beckoned me to follow the mustached man. I shuffled back out to the pacing and twitching bodies, over to a blood-dotted floor marked with colored lines.

We took the elevator to the seventh floor, a high-security locked ward. They let me in and took me to my room. Once there, my mind snapped like a chunk off a glacier. A whole lifetime of neatly stacked and tightly wrapped memories of guilt, rage and denial avalanched over me. I tumbled down inside myself to the very center of my right heel. Looking up, I squinted through the heavy but invisible agony. I saw that every orifice was blocked, packed in by unopened tintype pictures or sewn up by my own psychotic stitches. I felt like a pint-sized Thumbelina crushed down by the gravity of my unrecognizable pain.

Somehow I knew that I needed to sort through the photographs of each memory to find out when, where, and how I had lost myself.

3

Betty and Tiny

Memories, 1976

Martha, or Betty as she was called, was my mother. She was beautiful, with hair the color of wet tar, shaped in a blunt cut, slicked back short and tapered down. Her neck smelled like fresh marshmallows. She had gray eyes that twinkled, especially when others were looking. Her fingers tasted like Pall Malls.

I remember the spitting and wiping she used to do on my face; spit and wipe, rub, spit and wipe. Guess I was a dirty-faced kid. I liked to chew things, especially if they were growing.

Daddy would say with a knowing grin: "Robin, you know some dog or cow probably pissed all over that piece of grass."

So I'd stop—for a while. I sure did like the ooze of a thick stalk of roadside milkweed. But then I became a thumb-sucker. It was safer, much safer, because I always knew where that middle knuckle had been. I could wash

14

it, nibble it and roll it leisurely over my tongue or pull it out so fast you'd never think it had been near my face.

I can't remember my mama without dark lip rouge. The tube she used was glossy. I used to watch her put it on from the back seat. Standing way high on my tippy toes while keeping out of the way of her piercing gaze, I saw that she would smear the cherry blood on slowly, evenly, and, finally she would put a clean white tissue or piece of paper in her mouth, pinch down hard with her lips, and then "smush" it from side to side.

Sometimes when mom left two or three rouge lipped tissues on the floor, I would bounce over the front seat and collect the good ones. I'd take a whiff of the smell and then poke my finger through it's mouth. If it wasn't raining, the tissues made great kites out the back window. I'd keep one on my pointy finger till the wind tore it away. Sometimes it took miles and miles for them to be torn off.

I can still picture my mom's legs. They were like kissing snakes, softly wrapped and tucked neatly into her shoes. Other times they were like long, stretched-out hot dogs waiting to be boiled. Sometimes Mama was like those magazine bathing ladies that were tucked secretly under Daddy's front car seat—back deep, beyond far. Her gaze always seemed to be somewhere far off, thinking about other things. I would be standing next to her, and Mama would roughly brush unevenly my head, catching my ears every now and then. She was not mean; she just wasn't paying attention.

I could tell when she was dreaming. When she was, the brushing seemed like a lullaby taking her to another time, another place. She would drift further and further away, until suddenly she'd body twitch, and then she would lay the brush down, lean back, and stare at the emptiness in front of her. Finally, after what seemed like long, ticking minutes, Mama would stand, lean over me, and part my hair very carefully, just as if she were slowly cutting a piece of pecan pie. Then after two tugs she'd let-go and place a big floppy bow in my hair.

Sometimes Mama spit and pressed down on the stubborn loose hairs, and then she would give me a long look-over. I never knew if she liked what she had done. She'd just look at me, tilt her head from side to side, extend me out a full arm's length, nod, answer some question inside her head, shake her head in agreement, reach for her cigarettes, and then light up.

I never really knew what she thought of me, or even if she liked me. Sometimes when I had really bad earaches, she stayed up all night and rocked me, held me, and maybe even loved me. Sometimes I think the only time my mother could reach out and love me was when I was blanketed in pain: throbbing, pulsating, ringing pain. That was the only time I ever felt any warmth from her body or love from her heart. Somewhere, someplace inside, she must have loved me.

Martha Elizabeth Munn was born in Columbus, Georgia in 1926. Like my dad, she was the youngest of four. She was her stern Papa's beautiful little girl, a sweet and delicate Georgia peach. Betty could really twine men around her little finger with her drippy, magnolia ways.

Her Papa's family came from Paisley, Scotland. Mama mentioned in later years that I was related to John Quincy

Adams and the Newman clan associated with Paul Revere, who put the lanterns in that steeple in Boston, but I haven't traced any of my family history yet.

Grandpa Munn was a noncommissioned officer in World War I, in the horse artillery. He married his sweetheart, Leslie Pearl. Nanny, as I called her, had polio. I remember her metal brace and the big-heeled shoe she used to drag around her house so quietly. I don't think I ever heard her complain. She was so dainty and frail standing next to Papa. Papa was a walking voice: booming, cursing, and hand-rolled cigarette sucking. When I looked up at him all I ever saw were big spotted hands and a massive shiny head that seemed to scrape the ceiling. He was a great fisherman and hunter. He always wore a floppy hat covered with his handmade fish flies.

After I grew up, my mother's brother, Uncle Kenny, told me a little about my mom's life before I was born. He said that my dad, who was known as Tiny, married my mom out of friendship, and my mom seemed to have married him out of need. I have my mother's wedding ring. The thick, fourteen-karat gold band says, "To Betty from Tiny, Nov. 20, 1949."

My father's parents were Russian Jews. They came from a small village about two hundred miles southeast of Moscow. My great-uncles were farmers from Russia. Dad's family moved to the United States just before he was born. They settled in central Washington State near Dryden. At diners, I would hear a language I couldn't understand, see candles and smoke. I especially remember the sound of crunchy grass as I ran down the rows and rows of winter apple trees.

My father, Eugene L. Schillereff, was his mother's favorite. He was the last of nine and was born in Dryden, Washington, sometime in the late autumn of 1925. He graduated from high school in 1944 and enlisted in the navy right away. In later years, I always thought of him as a cross between Richard Boone in *Have Gun Will Travel* and Carl Betz on *The Donna Reed Show*. He had a coarse, gravelly, Fred Flintstone voice. He was a morning hacker, especially during his bathroom time. Dad was all cigarette wheeze and rolling lung congestion. His morning ritual was composed of grunts and flushes.

When I think of my father, I can only see parts of him or smell him although parts of him linger within parts of me. Until the time my parents divorced, when I was ten years old, Dad was the only person who ever gave me any sense of myself—who I was or who I might possibly be. When he asked, "How big is Robin?" I would reply, mimicking him, "So big." It was the biggest and fullest sense of myself I ever had as a child. I loved his ways of exaggerating a story. I loved the timbre of his voice as he sang along with the radio, or the way he would sneak me little presents and winks when Mama wasn't looking. I loved his glorious Cheshire cat smile and his beautiful white teeth. He wore glasses, but I don't really remember them on his face. My memories are of when he was drunk and couldn't find them or they were embedded in his cheek because of some fight; that's the only reason I knew about them at all.

His hair was brown, thick and coarse, with just a hint of a wave in front. When he was young, he was almost pretty in a kind of East European way. He had a lean leg;

a tight, firm arm; and a solid shoulder, but I can't seem to put all the pieces together, even now.

Later when I was in high school and only seeing him occasionally on the way home from school, he was still the consummate salesman. He sold everything from cars to rolling casters to beveled glass. People seemed to like working with him, and after his remarriage his bouts with sobriety grew longer and longer. His new wife Sheryl was strong and ran him and their whole household, which included my dad's three stepchildren. There was no more room for me in his new life, so I pulled myself away. I still loved him. I even liked him. But as the years wore on I realized how weak and sad he really was. Dependent would be the right word. Not even codependent. Dependent.

My father's feet stank to high heaven. It didn't matter how much he washed them or how clean his socks were. I guess it was some kind of perspiration thing. Maybe that's why I've always had such a fetish about keeping my shoes on—because of the fear that I might have inherited the Schillereff foot gene.

The last time I saw my father was when Eric and I visited Cashmere after we found my mother in Seattle, stoned on her ass, Christmas 1972. We talked on the phone a few times over the years. He sent a few birthday cards now and then when he could sneak them past his wife, the matron of the family. When I think about his physical appearance, he hangs suspended in my mind like a broken string puppet—bits and pieces, foot, head, leg, and arm. I don't have a full sense of my father like I do my mother. That seems strange because we were so close.

Robin Taylor

I wish I could put him all together and make him one person, but he was really always two people. One father was a happy, boisterous, cocky, fibbing, laughing, crying, salesman of a man who loved me very much. The other father was a whiny, sad, belligerent, mean, and hurtful man. I wonder if I'll ever understand why I loved him so much and not my mother.

My older brother was born on September 19, 1950, and given the name John Munn Schillereff. I came along on May 28, 1952. Robin Rae Schillereff. I was a blue-baby, born in a taxi en route to St. Joseph's Hospital in Tacoma, Washington. The hospital didn't think I'd make it. I was baptized and put in a incubator until my blood set, and I gained some weight. Tiny was working at the local prison then, but after a few months he was fired, something to do with him and the warden.

By the time I was better, about six months later, Tiny got a job as a county supervisor for a magazine subscription service. I was the daughter of a traveling salesman from 1952 to 1957. Three of those years were in a 1949 black Buick, and the other two were in a dark green 1954 Mercury. There were road motels, trailer camps, migrant shacks, jails, barrooms, and a few theaters.

4

❦

First Light

I knew Daddy didn't understand my replies to his
questions, so I just let him think there was no sense to
my gurgling drool. But I understood everything he was
saying, or at least I thought I did. Strange, flashing lights
whipped across his face and shoulders. When I tried to
roll over, I was stopped by a big, warm pressure down
near my tummy, where my other voice was. It made
me laugh as I was rocked back and forth on the car seat,
listening to the smooth sounds just beyond the black.
It must have been the car radio. Daddy used to mouth
along with the long sighs and hums. This was our time,
the night time, my Daddy and me, but it was also the
dark time, because of his arms, his fingers and the heavy
breathing behind me. Sometimes the ceiling would drift
away and all around and above would be winks of white.
I remember all these things so vividly. Sometimes there
was a *whoosh* sound and then moving air all around my

head and face. I felt as if I had been lifted up and out of the car. It was thrilling.

For several months, Daddy drove most nights and sometimes during long, bright days. Our car passed by thundering rivers that ate all sound, and rolling coastal hills that were better than car-seat rocking. Whispering fairy-like falls left soft wet kisses all over our cheeks and bottoms. Then, after the sky God had a good long cry and shook all over, we'd drive out onto the long, flat yellow. Nodding husk heads on crispy straw bodies waved at us as we passed by.

It was after that Mama first said to me, "We're takin' you home, Miss Jones. Mr. Jones is waitin' for you." From the back seat, I squirmed and tried to sit up and say, "No" but my tongue couldn't form the words. Mama turned around and nudged Daddy. Johnny cocked his shiny air rifle and shot through the half-opened window. The feeling in my throat was like a lump of bitter milk. I knew I was Robin Rae Schillereff. Who was Miss Jones?

For years, until I was too big, I slept on the floor next to the front seat with Daddy tucked up above me and Mama and Johnny sprawled out in the back. The carpet was worn out, so the old floor was blanketed with magazines and wrinkled state maps. When I drooled a lot or if my bottle fell, I might wake up in the morning with the imprint of the state of Virginia on my cheek or a fishing pole or trout tattooed alongside my arm. Some days were better than others, and we'd stay in dusty roadside motels. Some had bubbly faucet water; others had leaking showers. But the best had a real bed with pillows. Those early years seemed normal to me. It was how I thought everybody lived.

5

The Lost Mary Jane

Spring 1954

We were cruising smooth over a high mountain range. I had on a brand-new pair of Mary Jane patent-leather shoes. Daddy was happy. Mama was too. We had a little money to spend on things, fun things. We had bottles of Coca-Cola, a plastic bag of marshmallows, and sweet black and red cords of licorice.

Johnny was being a piss-ant, as usual. When we had a potty stop, he'd chase me and shoot the air rifle in my ears as I tinkled and tried to wipe. Back at the car Daddy said, with his arms outstretched, "How big is Robin?" I said, "So big," copying his arms over and over till we laughed and hugged. Then I hopped back into the car beside Johnny. Mama kept referring to me as Miss Jones this, or Little Miss Jones that, or just plain Cinderella.

Johnny made a threat to shoot me in the face. Then he ripped off my left shoe with a quick tug, and tossed it out his open window. All the while he pointed the rifle at my head and mouthed at me to hush. It seemed like hours went by; then, I started to cry. Johnny's sweet grin turned into mean threatening pouts as I cried louder and louder. Finally Mama turned around. "Stop that whimpering," she insisted. "Robin! Stop it! Stop it you two!"

With a choking voice, I blurted out, "Johnny threw my pretty new shoe out the car window!"

"What?" Daddy bellowed.

"Johnny threw my …," I stuttered but was cut off.

"Goddamn it!" Daddy slammed on the brakes and brought our 1949 four-door Buick, which we'd named Tallulah the First, to a crunching stop. Then he started swinging at Johnny behind him with his right hand, while shifting and turning the car back around with the other hand. "Where, where did you throw it, Johnny? Where is it?" Daddy asked as we headed back up toward the tall mountains.

We looked for my shoe until the stars were brighter than Tallulah's lights. We never found it.

Johnny got the shit beat out of him, and I liked that. As Daddy was busy whipping Johnny, I went around the car and found some pine cones for making a car box family.

Back in the front seat, Daddy let me play with the Texaco fire truck and locked Johnny's air rifle in the trunk. It was a good time. Daddy was still stewing hours later. I could tell by the way he smoked his cigarettes, sucking and blowing long and hard. Mama and Johnny went to sleep in the back seat. I tried to hug close to my door cause I was afraid of Daddy's slapping, angry hands. He seemed okay at the first gas station, so I got out to watch the gas being pumped. Daddy yelled at me, so I ran and jumped back into the car. The nice gas man shut my door. He looked like an old bleached raisin with wiry, kitty whiskers. He was funny.

We drove on and on that night. Lights came and went. I guess I fell asleep.

From the back seat, I heard Johnny yell out, "I gotta pee, Daddy!"

"What?" Daddy said.

"I gotta go, Daddy!"

I heard someone stir, and then a blanket touched the top of the seat. "Here use this, Johnny," Mommy drawled out. "It's empty. Just don't spill. Honey, drive real smooth so Johnny can tinkle, and we don't have to stop." Then she settled back down, taking the blanket with her. It got real quiet.

This was exciting! I stood up and looked over the seat. Way down below, Johnny was trying to pee in an empty Coke bottle. *Wow*, I thought, *neat*. Johnny tried to maneuver himself inside the bottle. After a quick bit, I heard the sound of a faraway fairy falls, then a tinkle noise, and finally nothing. Johnny tried to pull his "nunny" out, but it wouldn't turn or move around at all. The more he tried, the tighter it stuck.

"Ow, ouch, Daddy! MOMMY!" Johnny whined. "It's stuck! My nunny's stuck and it won't come out of the bottle." Then he started to cry big tears. That was really something, coming from Johnny. I started to feel bad for him, so I turned around and sat back down as Mommy sat up to help Johnny. "Darlin', he's really stuck in this thing, and I don't have any hand cream or lotion in the car. Tiny!" She tapped hard on Daddy's back shoulder.

Cursing under his breath, Daddy drove Tallulah off the road and then stopped. He threw open his door and got out, talking under his breath all the while. Tallulah's headlights were still on, because I could see the tree ghosts standing at the edge of her eyes.

Crunch, crunch, crunch. Daddy went around to the front of the car. There were noises, and the front hood lifted up a like magic carpet. Daddy came around to my side. It looked like he climbed inside, and then I heard, "Shit!" He must have bumped his head. Then he stood up, and in his hand was a long, thin stick. He waved it in the air like a magic wand and came around the front of the car and yelled, "Johnny, open that door!"

Johnny was still holding onto that Coke bottle dangling between his legs. Daddy pulled Johnny's legs over the edge of the seat, and ran his fingers down the long wand. It looked like Daddy had cut himself.

"Daddy's bleeding!" I yelled out. "Daddy's bleeding bad, Mama!"

"No, Robin," Mama said. "It's just the engine oil."

Daddy rubbed Johnny's pee-pee with the oil, and with three big breaths, his "nunny" slid out all greasy. The bottle dropped free onto the gravel below. I still remember the clink of that bottle. Then I felt the jarring shake of Tallulah's hood slamming down.

I liked it when Daddy sat down hard again because it made my body roll down into his. Later, standing up beside him, I watched with Tallulah's eyes as we passed tall, pine-tree people guarding the curvy road. Daddy said that one of the tree children was probably wearing my one new shoe, which made me feel better.

The next morning, I put the other Mary Jane under a bush, near the spot where I'd peed. I told it to walk on up the mountain and find the little tree girl who was wearing the other shoe, and I just knew that it would.

6

Turtles Don't Bleed Gray

Fall 1954

Standing on the dirt side of the pontoon boat dock, I watched as Papa Munn pulled green bowls from Lake Halawaka on the Chattahoochee backwater. Down on one knee with his back to me, he arranged them in a half-circle facing the lakeside of the dock.

I'd heard Johnny calling for me from Uncle Ben's cabin. He'd found a wasp's nest the day before, and now he wanted to throw rocks at it. I didn't think it was a good idea. So I snuck around the screened-in porch and crossed through the lightning bug yard to see what Papa Munn was up to.

Earlier, about an hour after Nanny's breakfast of fried catfish and grits, Johnny and I had gone swimming behind the cabin. This part of the Chattahoochee was a muddy red-brown. The water felt good on our hot bodies, particularly in the mouth-breathing, sticky heat. As we bobbed waist deep near the shore, we saw Papa Munn steering his motor boat back toward the dock. He'd been gone since before sun-up doing his morning fishing.

Excited to see what Papa Munn might have caught, Johnny and I climbed up over fallen logs and broken pine branches and across the mud embankment to meet him. He yelled at us from the docking boat, telling us to stay put. I didn't know what we had done, but I was frozen to my drippy spot. After tying up his dingy, he stepped up onto the planks. Then I heard him spit and felt him rubbing hard up and down the back of my legs. Papa Munn's hands were like sandpaper, and the rubbing really stung. While he did that to me, I looked over at Johnny and saw icky, gray slugs on his back and legs.

"Leeches," Papa Munn said. He used his tobacco spit to wipe and pull them off. When he was done rubbing and spitting on me, he started on Johnny. I watched. By the time he finished, it looked like Johnny had the chicken pox. After Papa Munn killed the last leech, we went off to play.

Mama and Nanny were napping, so we had to be quiet near the cabin. Johnny took off to chase something, and I was getting tired of blocking up red fire-anthills. I decided to go back and see what Papa Munn was doing. I didn't realize I had put my thumb in my mouth. It just felt so good to suck it and watch Papa Munn and all the boats speeding by.

Suddenly, Papa Munn stood up and yelled at me again. I had a hard time understanding him because of his accent, especially when he was angry, as he was now, at me! *Oh no,* I thought, as my mind whirled. He must have seen me sucking my thumb. Papa Munn always

29

threatened to cut it off at the roots if he ever caught me chewing on it again. He'd pull out his big hunting knife, which he said he made rattlesnake belts with, and say, "Robin Rae, you're gonna lose that thumb."

Now he'd caught me when I wasn't even thinking. I walked toward Papa Munn, ever so slowly, with my hands tightly squeezed behind me. Praying, I crossed over the pontoon planks. Then I saw it, the knife, Papa's long hunting knife. Red paint dripped from it. I looked down at where the drops landed and saw that all around Papa Munn's feet were the scattered green bowls I'd seen him toss earlier.

I saw now that they weren't bowls but little green turtles. Some of them were headless, squirming and lying in pools of bright red blood. Papa Munn stepped over them and walked toward me. He grabbed my wrists and dragged me back to the water end of the dock. Then he took my sucking hand and put it in a warm puddle of blood. The thick turtle blood seeped between my fingers.

"Are you gonna stop sucking your thumb, Robin Rae?" Papa Munn bellowed.

"Yes, Papa. Oh yes, Papa Munn," I said, crying and trying to pull my hand back. But the more I pulled, the tighter the knife cut my skin. I stopped fidgeting and fighting, afraid that if I didn't quit, I'd end up like the turtles, dead. When I finally convinced Papa Munn that I would never suck it again, he lifted me up, walked me to the back end of the dock and down the embankment, and put my hand in the muddy water. After he sloshed it and let go, I ran as fast as I could back to Uncle Ben's cabin.

There I hid, tucked up tight under the sagging mosquito porch cot until suppertime.

That night Nanny made turtle soup. I couldn't eat it. I just sat there and spooned at it. Johnny seemed to love it, and so did Mama, and Papa Munn. I just sat there and stared at the near full bowl. I knew that turtles and I didn't bleed gray.

7

Bourbon Street

Early Spring 1955

Big, smoky hands lifted me up and out of the corner, as I tasted the scent that was Daddy. Pressed snugly against his chest, I felt the rhythm of his walk. My eyelids fluttered as I tried to adjust to the bright table-lamp glow. Gently, ever so gently, Daddy laid me down on the motel bedspread. I could feel the cotton popcorn bumps under me and all over my sweaty skin. "How big is Robin?" I heard Daddy say from outside my closed eyes.

"So big," I answered, yawning and stretching and finally looking over at him. Crossing to the table, he turned around. "Where's Johnny and your Mother?"

"They're gone, Daddy. Mama's gone lookin' for you." I said, twisting around to see if my back and legs were dented from the popcorn bumps on the bedspread. I was glad Daddy was there to protect me; the sounds of the parade outside the window were getting louder and more raucous. With a twinkle in his eye, Daddy said, "Where's my favorite little girl's new party dress?"

"I don't have a new dress, Daddy. Mama threw out my old one. It's gone. I don't have a play dress," I said sadly, watching him fill up his glass.

Pointing with the bottle, he said, "Well, what's that hangin' over the side of the chair?" He smiled. "Maybe some good fairy brought it all the way out of China." Daddy laughed to himself and poured some more liquor into his glass. I started to get that bad feeling rising up in my stomach, but for the moment I forgot Daddy's drinking, slid off the bed, and ran over to the chair.

"Oh, Daddy," I said. "Is this really for me? Really?"

He nodded yes and sat on the edge of the bed.

"It's so pretty! It's the prettiest yellow dress I've ever seen." I ran over and gave him a big hug, almost knocking over his drink

"Daddy, why is the dress all bumpy like the bedspread?" I rubbed it on my face and between my fingers.

"Well," Daddy said. "The lady at the store called it Swiss bumps. No, Swiss dots. No, oh, what the hell? Oh yeah, she called it Swiss polka dots. You have a Swiss polka-dot dress, Robin, and it's very special. So special that I want you to put it on this very minute, 'cause we're going out." He took a long sip of his drink. Looking just past the rim of his glass, I saw a tall, green monster-head twirling by the window. Screaming, I covered my face.

Daddy nearly spilled his drink all over my new yellow dress. Turning, he looked to see what had frightened me. He laughed and crossed to the window. Opening the shutters, he said. "Don't worry, Robin honey. It's just a parade. It's called Mardi Gras. Those are just masks, and they won't hurt you. They're just havin' fun. Now go on,

33

put this dress on, and let's go out and get some supper, okay?" Daddy bent down and handed over my stiff, new, polka-dot dress.

"All right, Daddy." I walked toward the bathroom door, hugging my beautiful new dress. I let out a "yippee" when I got inside and a couple more when he didn't scold me.

After I dressed, Daddy picked me up. We went out through the two doors into the crazy crowd. I felt like a princess as Daddy carried me high over the street, pushing his way through all the people. When we got to the other side of the street, we stepped through a doorway. I noticed that there were two beaded necklaces around my neck, which had appeared as if by magic. Deep down inside, I knew that Daddy had something to do with it.

We stepped into a thick cloud of smoke and I had trouble seeing. The room had the same smell as Daddy's night breath. I saw ghosts moving with their cigarette candles, talking and swaying to tinny horn music. Daddy sat me down on top of a crowded counter. I heard "hi's" and "hellos" and a lot of deep-throated laughter. A skinny man pinched my cheek, and a lady with red lips said I was pretty. I felt so special, being there with Daddy and wearing the new, beautiful yellow dress. A bearded man from behind the counter said something to Daddy and he put me down on the floor.

I saw a room full of tables and chairs, and men dancing with ladies in tight skirts. I saw the flash of a funny-scooped horn, and a brown man rocking back and forth to the sweet, smoky music.

Daddy bent down and said, "Honey, that's a saxophone.

34

That's man's music. Come over here, and sit down." He grabbed a stack of papers and books. I noticed one piece of sheet music in particular. It was a picture of a beautiful lady with records around her face.

As he sat me down on his lap, I asked, "Who's that lady, Daddy?"

"Why, that's Lena Horne, honey. She's a wonderful singer."

Boy, did I feel special. Lena, that was a nice name. Maybe Mama would remember that one, I thought. Daddy scooted me up close to the table so I wouldn't spill food on my lap. The waitress had delivered a huge bowl with steamy chunks of meat and potatoes to our table. Daddy took his handkerchief and tucked it into my collar. Mmm, the stew smelled wonderful. I ate and ate while Daddy told stories at the counter, his hands flying. It was a good time.

I listened to the warm music and words and the laughter. Daddy was telling road stories. I knew they were mostly fibs because I had been there, but he was so happy, and everyone seemed to really like him. Daddy got louder and louder. I had my face down into the stew. Blowing and eating, I kept thinking to myself, *I don't think so, Daddy*. Suddenly, someone suddenly pulled back my chair, lifted me up, and put me down on the floor. I turned and looked into Daddy's face. He was beaming.

"Dance for me, Robin, dance," he said, all flushed.

There were chair legs in the way; they looked like a forest. But then, like magic, they were gone. My knees did some weird bending thing. I don't remember hearing the music, but I felt free and fairy-like as I turned in circles. I put my arms up like a butterfly's wings and got lost in the exertions of my private expression. I loved to dance, especially for my Daddy. My favorite part was when he lifted me up onto his shoes. I grabbed behind his knees, and we danced together between tables and chairs and way out into the space where the women in high heels swayed. I laughed because I was so full of love and joy, I thought I might burst. I don't remember how long we danced.

My next memory was getting undressed by Daddy back in the sticky motel. I guess I was tired, because I woke up with my arms straight up and my head being jolted when my dress collar got stuck under my chin.

"Ouch," I said from somewhere inside my dress.

Daddy tried to help me, but his hands fumbled. I slid off the wrinkled bedspread, landing feet first. My dress was on the floor, and Daddy was singing from somewhere in the bathroom. I loved to hear him sing, and the air was filled with his breathing. Mama and Johnny were still gone. When Daddy came back into the room, I told him I had to pee. He took me back into the bathroom, helped me pull down my panties, leaving them on the floor. Then he lifted me up, put me on the toilet seat, and went into the other room.

As I sat there tinkling, I looked down at my panties; they had a funny face that stared back at me. I tried to pull the toilet chain, but it was too high, so I slid off and wiped with my underwear. I was so proud of myself because I could take care of myself even when Daddy wasn't there. I walked out of the bathroom, naked except for my shoes and socks. I thought my feet were so ugly, I always tried to keep my shoes on. I even wanted to go swimming with my shoes and socks on, but Mama always made me take them off.

Through the window, the parade seemed slower now; there were only a few scattered masks and feathers walking by. The room was dark except for a glow from Daddy's Camel cigarette. He was in a low mood. He sat with his back to the window, his shirt open. I could see the glisten of sweat down his chest, which had hair lumps, all gathered, like little doll's heads. His motel glass was tipped over on the floor, surrounded by a brown circle of wet.

"Close the door, honey," he said. "The light hurts my eyes." He waved me toward him. "And bring that bottle over here with you," he muttered as he sank deeper into the chair's cushion.

The contents of the brown bottle were half gone. I could still reach it, so I carried it to him. Daddy's eyes sneaked open as I brushed his leg with the bottle. He took it and looked around for the glass. I found it next to the chair and handed it to him.

He said, "Thanks." His voice sounded so tired and far away. He poured another glassful and put the bottle between his legs. Then, with a hand, a sloppy hand, a whiskey-smelling hand, he stroked my damp hair. But I didn't care because it was Daddy's smell. The bottle was still between me and his stomach.

As I looked up, Daddy had a sad face. At first I couldn't tell if he was sweating or if those were real tears. But his voice changed to choking sounds and he almost crushed me to him as he rocked me back and forth. I cried because he cried, as he rocked me back and forth, back and forth.

He then spoke in a language and started to sing a song I couldn't really understand. My breath was caught between his shirt and his damp chest hairs. He reached to grab the neck of the brown bottle, and his hand was in my pee-pee place. It tickled, I laughed, but he didn't stop. He laid me across his legs with his big arm holding my chest and arms down. I tried to squirm away. I cried out: "Stop, Daddy, stop," but I only felt a pressure, hurting, way down inside. "Daddy, no, it hurts! I need my panties, my panties!"

A strange, glazed look came over his face. Then he reached for the bottle and took a long drink over me. His tight, lipped breathing puttered out and stopped. Daddy let the near-empty bottle fall.

Squirming, I fell off his lap and right onto the carpet where the brown wet spot was. Crying, I ran for the bathroom, but he was quicker than I was. He caught me like a loose piece of money and crushed me down onto the bed. Kneeling over me, my back pressed down on the bumpy bedspread, his wetness slid all over me.

The fireworks and shouts outside in the crowd covered my silent screams. There was pain and then a warm wetness. I jerked my head up from the bed and saw Daddy's face in my private place, my pee-pee place. He took the bottle; then there was pain. I must have peed because it was so wet, so warm. I don't know what happened next. I went inside. *Where can I hide? Where can I go? What did I do to hurt him so?*

I remember the bottle being tilted up and then a

stinging wet. Then Daddy's face was gone. My body fell back into the bedspread's popcorn bumps. Spiraling down into the thick wet blackness, I no longer heard the parade going by.

8

AA and the Route 66 Diner

Summer 1955

There were so many grownups walking and pacing back and forth in the smoke-filled room. I sat bottom-deep in a dirty sandbox, spooning for dead cigarette butts. Johnny was in a corner throwing "wall penny" with an older boy and pocketing sugar cubes off the refreshment table. I couldn't see Mama's face, but I heard her silky voice through the haze and knew exactly where she was sitting. I knew where she was because of the way she crossed and uncrossed her shapely legs. Daddy was somewhere in the other big room, where men said their names and were given a "Welcome," and "So glad to see you." It had the feeling of a tent prayer meeting, but these farmers weren't using those funny, high-pitched words.

Some kids younger than I was, still in diapers, crawled around on the ash-laden floor. There were tiny nose-pickers, open-mouthed squealers, and even some red-faced tantrum throwers too. I'd been having some bad earaches lately, so I kept my distance. I shoveled in the sand alone, rocking to the ringing inside my head. I tried to hear Daddy say his name in the other room, but I never did.

This seemed to be a meeting place where parents and other grown-ups could tell their stories and cry without feeling bad. Johnny got into a scuffle with the other "wall penny" boy. Then a really cute boy about Johnny's age came in with a skinny, gray-haired lady and crossed to the edge of the sandbox. Sitting on the side of the box, he watched me dig for a long while. Then he came on in, and we played together without speaking for what seemed like days and days.

Sneaking a quick look, I saw he had the longest lashes I had ever seen. There was also a small moon sliver of a scar on the downside of his mouth. It disappeared when he smiled. After we shared spoons, he showed me a cat's eye marble he had in his pocket. He even let me hold it. The glass warmed up with the heat of my hand. I wiped the sand off using my fingers and gave it back to him, blushing.

Suddenly, there was the sound of chairs being pushed back and big clopping feet walking toward us. I was so involved in burying my pile of cigarette butts that when I looked up to show the cute, little boy with the sliver scar my secret burial mound, he was gone. I saw the skinny lady and an ancient man wearing overalls go out through the main double doors. I guess my cat's-eye-toting crush went with them. All around me there was a forest of legs, like a curtain of stockings. I guess everyone was lined up to get coffee. There were rolled-down socks, shear hose held up with garters, and painted nails peeking through open-toed shoes. There seemed to be more moms than dads, and I saw them put cookies in their purses and snap them shut.

Afterward, back at the car, Daddy seemed to be in a good mood and so was Mama. She said that a woman told her that the Route 66 Diner was just down the road. It was supposedly a really good "chop house," Daddy said. He loved steaks, and I was really hungry and so was Mama. Johnny wasn't complaining; I guess it was all those sugar cubes he'd eaten.

"Shut your mouth, Robin, before the flies fly in," Mama snapped as she adjusted our chairs around the restaurant table. There was so much noise and activity. I didn't know where to look. I forgot all about my ringing ears in this room full of buzzing chatter. We were all there, tight against the table, Daddy, Mama, Johnny, and me. We sat next to a wall with paper leaves running up and down it. Daddy bought us all special drinks. Johnny and I had Shirley Temple drinks, Daddy had black coffee, and Mama had a brown drink with cherries in it. It looked cold.

Playing with the stiff leaves and vines, I peeked between the white slat fence and saw the cute little boy from the sandbox. He was on the other side of the partition, eating mashed potatoes and gravy, alongside the skinny lady and the stooped man in overalls. I felt a rush of hot blood to my cheeks and face when I caught him staring at me. I didn't realize I had been standing on my chair. I was in love. We exchanged private looks throughout the course of my drink and his mashed potatoes, and even through my greens and his cherry pie.

After a while, dinner finally came. Our waitress was dripping with sweat. My plate was covered with thick. gravy-covered meat. "Chops," Daddy said, sawing away at his. Mama helped me cut mine up. I was giddy and feeling flirtatious, so I took a really big grown-up bite without looking. I had a boyfriend now. I knew how to behave.

Without looking at my plate, I started to chew on my meat. I chewed and chewed. It seemed like the more I chewed, the bigger the meat got. I started to get a little nervous, but I didn't want Mama, Daddy, or my boyfriend on the other side of the vines to know I was having trouble. I looked down at my plate and kept chewing and chewing. After a while, my chewing turned to choking and then coughing, because no air was going in at all.

I caught Mama's gray eyes looking at me across the table, but I couldn't open my mouth. It was jam packed with shredded meat, filling every corner and blocking my swallowing tube. My head started to feel heavy. Mama jumped up and ran around the table toward me.

She shouted at Daddy. "Jesus, Tiny, she's choking! She's turning blue."

Running over to my chair, he lifted me up. Then someone else grabbed me by the ankles and held me upside down. They shook me and shook me while another hand kept whacking me on my back. Like a volcanic explosion, a huge mass of chewed brown meat shot out and landed with a sticky splat on one of the few white squares of the restaurant floor.

Instantly, the room went quiet, too quiet. All I heard was spoons and forks dropping on near-empty plates.

Daddy sat me right-side up and smoothed down my skirt. Mama was already in her seat, tucking in Johnny's napkin. Daddy tucked mine in and said "thank you" to the man at the next table. He slid me in close to the table again. I was so embarrassed that I couldn't eat anymore, so I just sipped my water. I looked through the vines at my boyfriend. He just kept looking down at his plate, and he slid his fork from side to side. I felt awful. I didn't feel like a giddy grownup anymore.

After a while, the restaurant returned to its usual noise level, and we could hear raised voices again. I just sat there, twirling my straw in my near-empty glass. My throat was sore, so I let Daddy have the rest of my big chop. Johnny rolled olives at me across the table and laughed. "I saw your underwear," he said. "I saw your underwear." Mama slapped him upside the head, and he settled down. Daddy ordered us both ice creams. We got our favorite, Neapolitan.

That was my first crush, the cute boy with the sliver scar smile, my first love. I met him at an AA meeting and lost him at the Route 66 Diner.

9

❧

Speed Trap

Late Summer 1955

One morning, the birds were singing and the two-lane gray road was shiny and filled with puddles. The strong smell of ripe peach trees was so thick you could almost wipe it off the tree limbs whipping on Talullah's roof.

Mama and Daddy seemed a lot better after we got a brand-new car, Talullah the Second. It was a dark green Mercury 54 with silver chrome. Johnny and I had a fuzzy cord across the back seat, which we used to drive along with Daddy. When he turned left, we steered left, and when he turned right, we leaned right. It was fun, and we didn't fall off the seat when we bounced either. The floor was clean and smelled of pressed new carpet. Daddy said we got the new car because he had an accident with a what he called a "bull cow." So the office sent him some "wire money." That's why it took so long for him to come get us in Memphis. It must have taken a lot of wire money, I thought, because this car was even bigger than

Tallulah the First. I didn't know who the real Tallulah was, but Mama sure liked her.

We stopped at a roadside diner and had some hot biscuits, grits, and gravy. Across the table, Johnny wiggled his front tooth at me. Back and forth, front and back, until suddenly it popped out and sank to the bottom of his milk. Mama used her spoon to scoop it out and wrapped it in a piece of torn paper napkin. Johnny demanded it back, but Mama said she'd hold on to it to make sure the tooth fairy would come and leave him a surprise. That scared me; I thought it was an awful idea. I was really glad when we finally finished our breakfast and got back on the road.

We hadn't gone far when a siren sounded behind us. Daddy slowed down and pulled over to the side of the road, cursing and swearing and chewing around the short end of his cigarette butt. Johnny cocked his rifle. Mama turned around and snapped, "Put that gun away, now!" Then she pulled out her compact to look at herself.

I heard a door close and saw a tall man in a tan shirt and a big brown hat come up to Daddy's window. He looked down at Daddy; then he looked at us in the back seat. The two men exchanged words and papers.

Daddy yelled something like, "What sign? What the hell are you talkin' about?" The back of his neck was got really red. I could tell Daddy was mad. Mama lit another cigarette and put on another layer of lipstick.

The tall man with the big brown hat gave Daddy a piece of paper, and in a voice with a twang, he said, "Follow me."

The man pulled out in front of Tallulah, and Daddy

began hitting the dashboard hard, really hard, saying, "This is a Goddamn speed trap, and I'm not gonna pay forty dollars." Soon he drove us away from the trees and out into a part of town filled with shacks and peeling white fences. Little brown faces ran alongside as we drove by. Black-spotted dogs chased our car's dusty tail till they became only invisible barks. In the middle of this town, we finally came to a stop. Daddy and Mama got out and followed the tall man with the brown hat. A much younger, skinnier man and the biggest low-eared dog I ever saw met them at the door. Johnny, of course, opened the back door and snuck out. I stayed so I wouldn't get yelled at or knuckle-whopped.

Soon I heard Daddy yelling something awful, and then I saw a chair fly out the front door and roll down the steps. Then there were sounds of a scuffle and iron clinking. Then there was quiet. I pressed my back up against Tallulah's new seat and tried to see where Johnny had gone. The window of the car was too high to see out of, so I put my knees under me and stood up. As I turned I saw Mama's face appear like instant magic at my window, and then she opened the door.

Mama said, "We're going to have to stay here a couple of days, honey, so come on in and let me show you where we'll stay. Johnny—where's your brother? Johnny? Where is he?" she asked, looking around. I shrugged and shook my head back and forth innocently to indicate that I didn't know. Then the skinny man came from somewhere around the back of the building, holding Johnny by the collar of his favorite striped shirt.

Inside was a big office, a cigar-butt smell, and the

constant jingle of keys. Daddy was in a room past the wood stove burner. He had his hands bent over his head and he stared down at the floor. But when I came in, he said, "Don't worry, honey, you'll get something to eat and, look, you and Johnny have your very own beds." He pointed in the direction of the next cell, sighed, and lay down. The bars felt big and cold. Mama lay down on a bed across from Daddy, and Deputy Bubba, the skinny man, put Johnny in with me.

Later on the policemen let us play with the dog. He was as big as a circus pony, with soft, kind, teary eyes. That night we had a picnic on the office floor—well, all of us except Daddy. There was fried chicken, greens, biscuits and gravy, milk, and some kind of sweet yellow pie. I think it was the best meal I ever had. Later we washed up for bed in the tiny bathroom, and they locked us in for the night. It felt so good to sleep on a real cot bed, all stretched out.

The next day they let Mama go and do the laundry. I stayed with Daddy, who tried to teach me card tricks and checkers. Johnny slipped out. He made some friends and managed to get to the south side of town, or so said Deputy Bubba. Mama was out for most of the afternoon, and the sheriff went in and out of the office a lot. The phone rang, people shuffled in and out, or peeked around the door and left.

Later on in the afternoon, I asked, "Daddy, would you unbutton me, please?" I asked wiggling.

"Why?" he asked and looked up and laughed, and then he pressed me to him while stroking my hair, "Robin, honey, you just lift your pretty little dress like this. That's what dresses are made for, to get to that special place, real easy, just like this." With that he lifted up my dress, put it into my raised hands, and started to peel down my panties. Suddenly I heard a chair squeak and a push noise, and the sheriff's stony face came around the office door.

"Need somethin' in there?" he twanged dryly.

"Yes," Daddy said as he smoothed down my dress. "Robin needs to use the toilet." The sheriff took out his big key ring and clink-thunk went the key into the big gray lock. Then he took my hand in his and led me out. He closed the cell door, and again thunk-clink went the key. I looked back at Daddy. He looked at me, winked, smiled, and then stretched out long on the cot with an "I'm going to take a nap," sigh. The sheriff, cigar in hand, led me to the outer office and the tiny bathroom.

When I was finished, he held me up so I could pull the chain, and he even gave me his hanky to dry my washed hands. Daddy was sleeping in his cell, so the sheriff let me sit in his big swivel chair and go round and round, and I even got to look at a tall picture book and point out the faces.

It was getting near supper time, and I was so hungry. Finally Mommy came back with a box of our clean laundry, smoking and showing off her newly painted fingernails. Johnny still wasn't back and neither was the dog or Deputy Bubba. Daddy ate dinner in his cell, and Mama, the sheriff, and I ate out on the porch.

When it was getting near dark, there coming up the road were Deputy Bubba, the big dog, and Johnny leading a little puppy on a rope. I got up to run down to meet them, but Mama caught my arm. Johnny asked Mama and

Daddy if we could keep the dog, but they said he couldn't. But we got to have him in the cell with us that night. The speed trap turned out to be a good time, 'cause there was fried chicken, a big low-eared dog, a puppy for a night, and my first real bed.

10

⟨⟨⟩⟩

Marmalade

Late Spring 1955

It was late spring in the high desert near Holbrook,
Arizona. We were going to be there for some time because
Daddy was working the southwest territories, or so Mama
said. Daddy put us up at the Navajo Motel instead of
Wigwam Village with all the stores. He said it was just as
good, and it was a lot cheaper.

After Daddy left and Mama had gone out shopping,
Johnny and I snuck over to the motel court to peek into
the teepee windows. We even played cowboys and Indians
around the big cement tents and the parked cars.

Johnny and I had been talking on and on for a long
time to Mama about getting a cat. We'd never been in
any one place long enough to own a pet. But now, after a
lot of whining and begging and with Daddy away, Mama
finally gave in. A migrant family lived in an abandoned
old truck on the other side of Wigwam Village, past the
railroad track. Johnny had gotten to know a few of the
boys his age and said that they were getting rid of some

kittens. I was so excited. Over the past few weeks, I had been saving change—money that I had found in the sand around the cafés and trading-post doors: pennies, nickels, and dimes, which were harder to find. I also had five quarters. Using all the money I'd saved, I bought some canned milk, hoping and praying that Mama wasn't telling a fib about getting a cat.

Johnny said there were only two cats left; both were boys, which really pleased him. One was a calico, and the other was an orange tiger. The next day, right after lunch, and after Mama had a nip or two, we drove Tallulah past the Wigwam Village, almost to the railroad tracks, and parked. I had a little paper box in my hand. We got out of the car, crossed the railroad tracks, and went over to where the Matthews family lived.

A big woman with a dirty apron and a very sweet smile greeted us. Some children hung onto her skirt, while two other boys ran up to Johnny holding two kittens. Mrs. Matthews introduced herself, as did my Mama. I was glad to see that Mama fit in and that her free and easy manner didn't come across as drunkenness.

What little fur balls they were. Johnny connected with the gray-and-black stripped one, but I only had eyes for the tiger, the little orange fluff-ball with white, white stripes. One of the older boys put the little orange one right into my hands, and those gold-flecked hazel eyes just stared, not at me but into me. He fit so perfectly into my sweaty hands. He didn't even squirm, unlike Johnny's, which was attacking his nose. It looked like Johnny's eyes would be the next thing to be attacked, but the orange tiger and I were nose to nose, judging and searching.

I knew one thing; no kitten of mine would ever be called anything as common as Tiger. It was going to be named something special. It would have to be a name I really loved. That's when I looked at the kitten and decided, "Hmm, Marmalade."

By then Johnny's choice had clawed down his leg, leaving thread tracks all down his pants before rushing off into the abandoned truck. S, it was a unanimous vote from Mrs. Matthews, Mama, Johnny, and me; it was going to be the marmalade tiger.

We said our goodbyes and said we would let them know from time to time how he was doing. Mama gave Mrs. Matthews the hotel's phone number, since we didn't have a phone in our motel room. I was glad she did. In any case, we could always run over with a note to let her know how he was doing.

Waiting at home for us was a vast assortment of canned goods. There was probably a month's worth, so Mama couldn't complain if a little milk went missing for Marmalade. Our motel kitchen was really quite small, but with Daddy in the next county pushing his magazines, Marmalade settled in well. I made him a special little kitty-box from boxes from the A & P and the Indian market. I searched through all of them till I found the cleanest and most perfect size for a kitten. Marmalade made himself right at home.

Johnny soon forgot about him and went off, getting into trouble as usual. Mama went back to her naps and coffee-nip sessions with Mrs. Mills, who ran the Navajo Motel with her husband. Most of my time was spent with Marmalade.

I finally had something that was mine, something that fit as well as my first winter coat with the fake-fur trim, or like the way I felt at Nanny and Papa's where they had the best food ever, the perfect cookies and holiday fudge. That's how it was with me and Marmalade; it was the perfect fit. We were one. He was so cute. And he was a smart little devil. He followed me everywhere and got into everything that I was trying to do, or undo.

One time, Marmalade and I finished a string fight. Mama was gone, and Johnny was out playing war with two little kids. I climbed up on Mama's bed because I was pooped. Marmalade clawed his way up the faded orange bedspread, and then he walked over my legs and up onto my stomach. There he sat, purring as I stroked his fur from the tip of his ears down to his little white-tipped tail. We stared at each other, long and hard, until I finally saw his eyes droop. He had grown so big after only six days. In the back of my mind I remembered Mama saying not to let him fall asleep with me because he was so small. I kept my eyes open wide and listened to the traffic that rumbled or screeched by the window.

The heat formed little beads across my forehead and under my nose, so I tried ever so carefully not to tilt my head back and disturb Marm. That was his nickname, Marm. Then the drips rolled, merging into streams, and I had to shut my eyes against their hot sting. I squeezed my lids real hard till the salt blended and my eyes became numb. Then ever so gently, I relaxed my eyes. In doing so I guess I also relaxed my body. The car noises began to grow distant, and the room seemed to get cooler. I was only aware of the sound of my heart beating and my breathing, which matched Marmalade's. It was a good feeling, a quiet feeling. It seemed to last forever, but then suddenly the quiet was disturbed by a faraway muffled cry.

"Huh!"

My eyes shot open, and I felt a lump and something squirming under my back. It was Marmalade. *How silly of him to crawl under me*, I thought. I jumped up because my throat was really dry from all the heat. I walked to the kitchenette, and I looked back and saw Marmalade following me off the bed. I turned and filled up a motel glass with foggy tap water and crossed back to sit on the edge of the bed. As I started to drink, I saw Marmalade walking toward me, his head sort of cocked, dangling off to one side. He was swaying, the way Mama did around dinner time or like one of those head-bobbing toy dogs in the back window of a car. Marm opened his mouth and let out this deep purr, a sound I'd never heard before. It was a deep belly purr that turned into a scream. It was a sharp cry, a cry that grew louder and louder with each hobbling step. He just kept coming at me, screaming.

"Help me! Help me!" he seemed to be screaming.

The glass fell from my hand as I rushed to help Marmalade, but he didn't seem to recognize me. He just kept trying to walk, and he looked at me, pleading. He couldn't get off the bed, so I lifted him and put him down on the floor. His head still bobbed, and his eyes interlocked with mine, as he fell to his side.

I covered my ears, screaming. "I'm sorry. I'm sorry. I've hurt you, I've killed you! I've killed you!"

He lay there, trying to cry, blood coming out of his

55

mouth and nose, his legs paw pawing the air. He finally coughed a gurgling sound. His back legs twitched, and then he looked so tired. I stood frozen over him, like a human casket. He was choking on his own blood. I don't know how long I stayed there beside him: his friend, his parent, his executioner.

It was almost dawn when I took one of Mama's good hankies and put it in his box. I lifted him up and took him outside. There was only asphalt around the motel, so I walked down the road, past the Wigwam Village, and over by the railroad tracks where the dirt was soft. With a rock to dig the grave, I buried Marmalade.

It was just as well, Mama said. Daddy came back the next day, and we couldn't stay any longer due to something about Phoenix and the police. We packed up Tallulah and left the next day. I never told Mrs. Matthews about the kitten. To this day, marmalade is the only type of jam I cannot eat.

11

❧

Picking Cotton

Fall 1955

Copying the style of skinny Washington Jackson, I slid on my belly along between the fresh-picked cotton rows. "Look out fer dem spitting bugs," he told me, pointing to a sticky wad of fizzle-spit. "It'll blind yo' eyes till ya can't see nuthin'. And sting!" He pointed to a switch stick and said, "Look!" But I didn't see anything, so I just shook my head, kept watching, and scratched at my prickly arms.

"Keep lookin,'" said Washington. He was a little taller than Johnny with three front teeth a missing. He snapped back a branch, and then I saw it move, long and thin with stick grapping legs. Sure enough, just like Mama said, it was a tobacco-spitting spit bug. I stared and stared at it, while Johnny tossed dirt clumps over onto us from another row, laughing. We were supposed to be helping Mama out and fill our dragging sacks, but Washington Jackson had so much to show me that I just plain forgot.

After I sneaked by that one pissed-off spitting bug, I reached in ever so carefully to pull out the bulging cotton buds. Mrs. Jackson was way on up ahead bent over. I could tell by her shading hat and yellow-print skirt that it was her. She was so nice. The night before, after supper time, after Daddy drove off with Mama, Mrs. Jackson sang and sang, rocking me in her big smoky arms, way long, even after I stopped crying.

Johnny had made friends right away with Washington Jackson, and they ran off to play. I was left with Mrs. Jackson and her five other "chillun." One was even younger than I was and slept in a rocking box. It was the first time I saw a mommy's teat give milk. Mrs. Jackson said that was how she fed all her chillun until they had teeth and could chew on their own. I felt inside my mouth. Yep, I had teeth. I had a feeling I was too old for titty milk.

Outside the one-room shack was an open step where the Jacksons' skinny dog, Jarvis, slept. Mrs. Jackson said it was the coolest place, and since he was "up near close to God years," he deserved the best spot. But I also saw some of the younguns slide under that step, especially during the heat of midday.

Johnny and I lived with the Jacksons for almost a week. Mama said Mrs. Jackson used to work for her family long before Johnny and I were even an idea. Daddy and Mama were going to Mobile, Alabama, so they thought this would be the best place for us to stay, play, and learn about picking cotton. I even liked the picking part. Helping Mrs. Jackson make grits and biscuits over a fire, taking the laundry out of the cooking pot, and hanging the laundry on the line that stretched from the shack to the electric pole was fun. I didn't like the stinking outhouse, though, because it was filled with spiders. Johnny showed me a big daddy longlegs that he said bit his butt, and then he proceeded to pull off the legs, one by one. I couldn't watch the torture, so I ran into the folds of Mrs. Jackson's apron and clung to her till my eyes were dry.

I loved spending nights under the hanging porch net. I could hear the buzzing skeeters trying to eat me, but as long as I didn't roll into the net edge, I was be safe. My favorite time was the singing time. I especially like Mrs. Jackson's deep-chested hum. She would hold five of us chillun inside her big, soft, rocking arms and sing, humming and telling us stories. The one I remember the best was about a boy named Joseph who was thrown into a hole by his brothers. Johnny liked that one too, and for the next few days he would call me Joseph and scare me by saying he was going throw me down the outhouse hole, where I'd sink through the poop and down into spider hell. Mrs. Jackson said, "Don't pay him no never-mind. He's just playing at being a brother. They do those kinda things to their sisters." With that, she slapped Johnny upside the head just like I'd seen her do to Washington. I sure did like Mrs. Jackson.

The hard part on those hot afternoons was the picking off the dry, hard shells and sticks left over before the older men tied up the scratchy sacks of cotton. I sure liked doing what Mrs. Jackson did, though. She taught me real good. She taught me about titty-feeding babies, how to wash and hang sheets, and especially the wonderful feeling of hugging love.

Mrs. Jackson always said, "There's always enough huggin' love to go around for all of God's chillun."

She was my guardian angel. Whenever I made Daddy or Mama mad, I would close my eyes and feel her big soft arms go tight around me, hugging me, making all the evil go away. I would bury my face in the folds of her memory for many years, where I was hidden, concealed, hugged, and secretly protected.

12

Candy Jars

Winter 1955

A peeling, hand-painted sign hung outside the three-story brick building. The lobby had the same toilet-water smell as Nanny and Papa Munn's house did during the spring rains. It was a damp mixture of lily and sweet lavender, a pungent scent, an old person's perfume.

Two withered women with mothball breath greeted Johnny and me. They each stooped over and held out a glass candy jar. The tall glass had pretty colored jellies, and the short, wide jar had chewy, sugared orange slices. We both looked at Mama, and she nodded yes. Johnny went for the gummy fruit, which I hated, and I dug a fist into the multicolored jelly beans. Holding the candy under my nose; I caught whiffs of grape, cherry, and my favorite, black licorice. I knew I was going to like it here.

"Are they grannies, Mama?" I asked, my mouth full of the colored juicy.

"No," Mama said, and then she smiled as she spit-wiped my dribbling chin. "We're going to stay here with these lovely and kind ladies till Daddy gets back from his important trip. Johnny, stop that! Put it down!" Then she turned to me again and said, "Isn't that wonderful?" The wrinkled sisters nodded at each other, and then they looked down toward us, smiled, and then double-nodded again.

I guess we were out of money. Mama was so sticky sweet and nice. After their last fight, I didn't know when Daddy was coming back. He said something about "wire money" and sped off into the white rain. Johnny and I were taken up the carpet stairs by the two old women and told to stay in the two big rooms. Mommy was going to help out at the desk and would be back around bedtime. She left Johnny in charge.

The first room had scattered rugs, upon which were thick table feet. There were high marble dresser tops with hanging scalloped edges and wine colored pillows that coughed dust when we punched them. There was also a beautiful rose fabric lampshade with sparkly tears on the bottom. Johnny spun it around and around. I tried to catch the light reflections—they looked like stars—but they were too fast for me.

The other room had a gargantuan bed, but it was too high for me to climb on. The bathroom had a cold white floor, and the tub sat on funny birds' feet. Johnny and I didn't like that room much, so we played in the big room.

Things came open or caught our eyes. I found Mama's lipstick and decided to draw. Johnny liked cords and plugs and found an old iron. I filled in the fancy lace on the arms and backs of the velvet chairs, while Johnny made smoking animal tracks across the patterned carpet and floor.

That night Johnny and I got hairbrush spanked by Mama over the bird-footed tub. We really made her mad. The next day we moved to a church mission center. That was when the first real snowstorm I ever remember happened. It was in downtown Hartford, Connecticut, and I loved every inch of it. As we bundled up and left the wrinkled sisters' motel, they came out and stopped us. The day before they had been really upset with Johnny and me, but this morning they were different. They wore fingerless mittens. Just like before, they offered us candy from the glass jars. Nodding in unison, they told us we could each have two helpings. Mama said okay, and so we did. Johnny chose those icky orange things again, and I took the little jellies.

Daddy found us at the downtown mission about a week later. I still had one jelly bean left, hidden in a sock, saved special. It was the little black one, licorice, my very, very favorite. I saved it just for Daddy.

13

The Polio Shot

Late Fall 1956

We were staying at Nanny and Papa Munn's house for about two weeks, while Daddy traveled around Montgomery, Alabama. It wasn't Sunday, but we went to church anyway: Mama, Johnny, and me. As I ran from the house to the big black Pontiac, the uncut grass in Papa's front yard tickled just below my knees.

Johnny pulled up on the big silver handle to open the car door, and I climbed onto the warm front seat. I started butt bouncing. "Robin Rae. Stop that!" Mama snapped as she scooted in under the steering wheel and slammed the door. She wasn't in a good mood that morning. I settled down and pressed my back low against the deep plushy seat. Johnny sat up tall on his side, and he rolled down his window. The next-door neighbor's Pekingese dog started to bark. Johnny shot some spit balls at him. He had some ready in his pocket. Mama popped the car into gear, loudly, and then turned around and looked back over her shoulder. The big

Pontiac started to roll backwards, so I stretched my legs out, long and pointy, trying to touch the dashboard. My pink socks and dirty Buster Browns hung in the empty air. When the car started moving forward, I tucked my shoes up under me and sat up tall like Johnny so I could see better.

The ride to First Baptist Church was fun. There was lots to see—green lawns, pretty houses and streets, beautiful trees with big, open flowers.

"Magnolias," Mama said.

I loved the name and the hugeness of them. "Magnolias," I said, pointing excitedly out my open window, alerting Mama and Johnny to my every discovery. Mama would smile sometimes, nodding and clicking her gold wedding band against the black steering wheel.

It was a smooth ride. Johnny practiced his spitball shooting, and I stared out the window, smelled Mama's perfume, or sucked my thumb quietly. Cars in a variety of colors lined the streets on both sides of the church. Mama parked about a block away. The sun was really burning down, and I could feel the hot cement through the soles of my shoes. We passed the white front columns and walked around to the church's side door. Outside was a line of mothers and kids, mostly little, my size. There were a lot of kids like Johnny too, some with their front teeth missing. Mama led us over and by the time we joined the line, it had moved just inside the church's basement. I was glad because it meant the sun was off our hot necks. I didn't know anybody, but everyone seemed to be on their Sunday-best behavior. *Why were we here?* I thought. It wasn't Sunday. There were no pretty dresses, shiny Mary Jane shoes, stiff crinolines, or little boy bow ties and pressed short pants.

Inside to our left was another door, from which other mothers and kids came out. The children's faces were a blotchy red; some were almost the color of white hopscotch chalk. Others bit their lips, and their mothers fussed all over them, unrolling their sleeves and opening their buttons. *Hmm,* I thought to myself as Mama, Johnny, and I stepped into the cool darkness. Soon my eyes adjusted to the darkness, and, I could hear voices beside me.

"Oh!" I gasped. A lady skulked behind a table. She had on a white pointy hat and black-rimmed glasses. I think she was old but I couldn't see her face very well. She and Mama spoke for awhile, and then Mama signed a yellow sheet. While she was doing that, I looked around the legs and big skirts and saw a long snake of people. There were lots of children but mostly mothers. There were two Dads too. The winding line crept forward. My hand was sweating, so I wiped it on the bib of my overalls.

"Stay here, Robin, honey," Mama said and took off to find Johnny. She always added "honey" when we were in public. I looked around to see if any grownups had heard her say it, but there was no sign that they had. A fat kid Johnny's age picked his nose and ate it right in front of me.

I saw Mama in front of the hall, pulling Johnny away from a different table. He had something in his hand. Mama took it away, gave it to a lady in a white coat, and dragged Johnny back to where I was standing. My spine started to feel creepy, like when you hit your elbow and can't do anything but wiggle and shake. It felt pretty tense. Something was not quite Sunday right about this line.

"Tis! Tis!" Johnny shouted between Mama's pushes and shoves. He couldn't say "sis" because of his missing front teeth. "They got sharp pointy needles, and they're going to stab us," he said with a wicked grin. Johnny knew how scared I was of needles. Slowly, a throw-up feeling started in the pit of my stomach. The room seemed to turn to rubber, and the fat kid started to get on my nerves. A girl's face went red as she turned away from the white coats. She had a pinched, sour expression and wet cheeks. *Oh no*, I thought, looking at her hard. *Why was she crying? Was this going to hurt?* I knew something was up. My mouth got dry and dropped open as I turned around to see where we were in line. We were about six parents from the white coats and the table.

Bug-eyed, I stared at the fuzzy-haired girl, who was being fussed over by her hanky-waving mom. They peeled away from the end of the table. I could see a man in a white coat with even a balder head than Papa Munn's. He didn't look very friendly. He was stiff, just like the pastor during his long, yelled talks. Searching the faces of the other kids, I realized that I should be scared. There were dry screams, bottom-lip pouts, and lots of "ooh, ooh, NO! OUCH!" We were getting closer and closer. Mama was talking to the fat kid's mother in front of us, and the boogie-eater was sucking on a lollipop. I guess he stayed quiet as long as he had something in his mouth.

Whatever was going on at the near table, I thought, *it was not gonna go on with me.* I could tell it was going to

67

be something awful. My face started to get tight. Johnny sat on the floor, playing soldier, shooting the rest of his spit wads at the kids near the table. I turned back around and looked at all the other mommies and kids waiting patiently. They weren't wiggling; they were respectful, just like the first day of Sunday school. My heart started to beat hard. I could feel something in the back of my throat. Then without warning, from someplace deep inside me, low rumbling wails near my tummy came from my mouth. Then sobs and deep, booming convulsions shook my entire body. The hall's silence began to crack. My high-pitched screams headed toward the ceiling. The wails and sniffles of others soon followed.

Mama was real mad at me. She pushed me toward the woman in the white starched dress and jerked my left sleeve up. Mama tried to talk to me, but I wasn't listening, even though I knew I would get it when I got home. I couldn't help it.

Johnny joined in with some Indian yelps and did a fire dance around the now-screaming, lollipop-sucking fat kid. It was like a devil's chorus in the basement of the First Baptist Church that day.

A glint of silver caught my swollen eyes. I saw rows and rows of trays and pointy needles and cotton. The nurse stood me right in front of the bald doctor. My right hand grabbed the table and I looked back at Mama; somehow, I caught the edge of one of the trays. In a flash, instruments went flying, needles went rolling, trays went clanging, cotton balls went floating, and the room erupted into volcanic screams.

The floor looked like someone had kicked the tip

off an anthill. I felt Mama's hands planted firmly on my shoulders. The doctor picked up some of the scattered equipment and needles. Then out of nowhere, from behind, the nurse stabbed me. I felt the needle's point. It didn't hurt as much as I thought it would. Johnny got stabbed, too, but he stood firm and stuck his tongue out at the doctor.

Mama pushed Johnny and me toward the far door. That's when I noticed the line of kids and Mommies was no longer orderly but more like a snake trying to wriggle out of its skin. All the boys and girls were red-faced and were being dragged and slapped to the front of the room. I felt a certain stillness and calmness as I left the basement of horrors. I couldn't understand why everyone was so upset.

Later when we got back to Nanny and Papa Munn's house, Mama let me know. I had to go outside and pick a nice, long switch from the backyard bushes. It couldn't be brown, but had to be green so it could bend and not break. I guess I really embarrassed her a lot. That's what happens when you go to church on the wrong day.

14

Paper Christmas

December 1956

There were lots of stairs. Mama and Johnny were gone. Daddy was messing with the newspapers near the table lamp and had spread them out all over the bed. The sign across the street was blinking red then green on the ceiling above him.

I had finished my soup and "sannie," so Daddy helped me change and wash up. While I worked at my buttons, he moved a chair next to the double window. Daddy rolled up his woolly gray coat, took a pillow off the bed, smashed them both together, and placed them down hard on the chair. He lifted me up and sat me down tall, so I could see out and across the way. "Here you go, Robin," said Daddy, while he snapped a candy bar into five pieces. "I want you to eat these real slow and practice your counting, Okay?" He winked and put the chocolate along the cold cracked sill.

"Oh, Daddy, yes, Daddy," I said nodding excitedly as I reached for the nearest piece. Daddy brushed back

my hair with his smoky hand and then crossed back to
continue what he had been doing.

Down below, people in lots of ear-flapped hats and
long colored scarves hurried past. Boys with big brown
gloves dragged fat, prickly trees behind them. Faraway,
dogs barked. Church bells rang out, high and long.

The melting squares took a long time to eat. I licked
each one real slow, just like Daddy said I should, until it
was like a pancake, using my palm as a platter. Then I
cleaned each pointy fingertip and thumb. *Umm, good*, I
nodded to myself.

Starting through the window made my nose cold. I
blew misty shapes on the window pane to try and warm
it up. When my breath marks faded, there were little
chocolate circles all over the glass. I turned around to see
what Daddy was doing. He had long paper tubes piled
and scattered at the end of the bed. He was singing out
loud. I turned back to the window and started to lick off
the chocolate with my warm wiggly tongue. It tasted
different, but I ate it anyway.

"Watch this, honey," Daddy said.

I turned back around and climbed down off the chair.
He took a drink of his smelly brown water and waved me
over. I crossed to the bottom of the bed and wiped my
sticky hands on its blanket. Daddy reached down toward
the floor and into his open black traveling bag. He dug
around and pulled out the "Don't touch those" scissors.
He put them on the table next to his glass. Then he leaned
over the bed and rolled all the newspaper tubes over to
where he was sitting. I walked around the bed and stood
next to his open knees.

71

Daddy grabbed a paper tube and the scissors and started making cuts all around the top. When he finished, he put it down on his other side, closer to the table. He took a sip, and made snip, snip, snips on all of them. Then he took them all in both his hands, holding them like a long bunch of flowers.

"Do you know what this is, Robin?" Daddy asked me, shaking the paper canes.

"No." I reached out to touch one, feeling the paper tighten under my grasp.

"It's a pole," Daddy said.

"It's not a pole," I said, shaking my head and laughing at funny Daddy.

"Oh, but yes, it's a special pole. Watch!" Like a carnival magician, he began to pull up on each tube, one at a time. The cut edges fell like leaves as the canes grew and grew a zillion times bigger than their size. Then Daddy took some old magazines and shoved them inside an empty saltine tin.

"Find me Johnny's marbles," he said.

I ran over to our play bag. It was over by the closet door next to the dresser with the big knobs. In that bag we kept our Sky Chief Texaco fire truck, Johnny's click guns, my pine-cone family, some favorite rocks, and my only doll, a little navy sailor doll that Daddy gave me after I'd made him mad one time. Mr. Navy. He was carefully wrapped in a light blue towel. I always made sure his eyes were covered during the yelling times, the bad times. This was a good time, I could tell, so I took him out of his towel and kept him with me.

Digging around in the bag, I finally found the jar

of cat's eyes and other colored marbles that Johnny kept securely roped in an Ovaltine tin.

"Here, Daddy," I said, tipping the can back and forth and listening to the glassy marbles roll. I kept it moving while I walked across the room. He took the tin from me, untied Johnny's special knots, and poured the marbles into the tall cracker can that held up the newspaper tree.

"There," Daddy said. "That'll hold 'em." Then he turned back to me, smiling. He could fill up the whole room with his grinning teeth. "Honey, this year we're having a paper Christmas!"

"A paper Christmas?" I asked, tucking my doll up closer around my neck, so we both could hear better.

"Yep," Daddy said, turning back toward the table and picking up his almost-empty glass. "A damn, great, special, wonderful, just you and me, kid, Christ, holy, goddamn paper Christmas!" He finished his drink, stood up, and in two big steps was around the corner of the bed and heading toward the dresser. With his foot he pushed the play bag against the wall and stood with his back to me in front of the high hanging mirror. I couldn't see his face, so I leaned on the edge of the bed holding Mr. Navy and trying to see what he was doing. There was a kissing glass sound. It was the brown water again.

"Robin," Daddy slurred while looking at his reflection. "Paper Christmas." He stopped and took a long sip from his refilled glass. He turned around and stared down at me. "Paper Christmas means you cut out pretty colors or rip any magazine thing you want, and pin it or tie it on the special paper tree. Then next year or sometime when you're much older, all the things you want, come true.

73

They happen right and perfect just like you remember on that special night. Christmas night, with the paper Christmas wishin' tree. And that's why I call it paper Christmas."

Daddy dug into his travel bag beside the bed. "Now, Robin, honey, you must either cut out pictures of things you want, or draw them. I know I've got some extra colored pencils and pretty magazines in here somewhere. Damn! Oh, here we go."

"Will Mama and Johnny have a paper Christmas too?" I asked, reaching for the paper and pencils.

"Nope," he said. "They've gone to your mother's daddy's house. Papa Munn, good ole Papa General Lee Munn." Daddy laughed hard and slapped at the bed. "No, your brother Johnny and Betty, your mother, are having a regular Christmas, not special, not magical, just average. No, below average. We have the magic. We have the secrets." With that, Daddy tossed the wrinkled brown water sack at the door. Wham!

"Will our paper wishes really come true, Daddy?" I asked, my eyes busting wide open. They were open so wide the room took on a pinkish glow.

Daddy yawned. "They sure will, honey. Here, start drawing or if you want there's some magazines in my black bag. You can use the big scissors too; just don't cut yourself. I don't want to hear your mom nagging at me, so be careful now. Pick the prettiest things you want." Daddy lay down on the bed, stacked the pillows, and sipped at his drink.

I pulled the paper, pencils, and Daddy's travel bag closer to the double window for better light. I could only cut when the red and green lights flashed. I felt special cutting with the big "don't touch those" scissors. On one sheet of empty paper, I drew a picture of a beautiful, red, tall house. I cut out pictures of fish from some of Daddy's hunting magazines and put them in its yard. Then I put them on the paper Christmas tree instead. I poked holes in the paper with my pencil and pushed string through. Daddy showed me later how to tie them onto the tree. Then he lay back down and started to snore again. His now-empty glass was clenched between his long fingers; it rose up and down on his stomach like a bullfrog waiting for a fly.

The colored lights looked pretty through the double window. Mr. Navy watched everything I did. He chose the blue and some animals and one fish too. I looked over to show Daddy my drawings, but he was breathing real loud. He looked like a naked Santa Claus, without a beard. His cheeks were puffy and rosy and his hair looked like a funny floppy hat against the pillow. The room was dark except when the blinking lights stayed on for a while. Turning to pick up the scissors, I looked up and saw that Daddy's eyes had popped open and his breathing was quiet. He stared at me, his eyes damp and empty.

I quickly turned back to my pencils, trying to erase myself from the room. "Daddy can't see me," I said in my head, "Daddy can't see me," but I felt his eyes on my back.

"Go to sleep, Mr. Navy," I said, covering him with paper and then pushing him against the wall. "Go back quiet. Sleep. Shut your eyes."

I heard the bed springs creak. I pushed myself down

into my pretty red tall house. Out where the paper fish lay. I was behind the fence, out back, running, running toward the cut out mountains. The blinking red and green lights had stopped. I couldn't breathe. Hurry, hurry paper Christmas, hurry.

15

∞

Ballard Birthday Party

May 28, 1957

Between the time I flunked first grade and started attending the Hearing Institute on Capitol Hill in Seattle, Johnny, Mommy, and I lived for a short while in Ballard, Washington. The green duplex was one of many along the unpaved dirt road just above the canal locks. It was near an ice-skating rink.

For my sixth birthday, Mama invited a lot of nose-picking kids I didn't even know. That was okay, but I felt a little uncomfortable in my new birthday dress. It had big red and white polka dots all over it and a shiny black patent leather belt. It was so stiff I couldn't bend over to scratch my knees. Mama and Johnny had been blowing up balloons in the kitchen. On the counter was a store-bought box. Mama showed me a pretty white and pink cake hidden inside. The whole thing was too high for me to reach and touch, but I could see some leftover icing on the edges of the carton. The cake was just waiting for me to eat. It was going to be a wonderful party, I just knew it.

Because Johnny popped more balloons than he blew up, I took his place inflating the balloons. Johnny let one go as he went outside to play. It farted all around the room and landed on the edge of the coffee table. I remember that this happened after lunch because we'd had tuna sandwiches with pickles just the way Daddy liked them at least an hour before. I wished Daddy had been there to have some birthday cake and ice cream with me. He did promise me to bring me a really nice present when he returned from Yakima. Mama said the party would start in the afternoon.

I went out to sit on the porch step and wait for all my presents in my new big dress. It was pretty hard to breathe though; the belt was too tight. I sat up real tall and watched as all the strange kids with their big-haired mothers crossed over to our lawn. Johnny ran around and gave all the kids a balloon. Most of the mothers tied the strings on their wrists or button loops so they wouldn't lose them. There were three heading up to God already. Some of the older boys had balloon fights, popped them, and dragged them all around the yard.

My bottom started to get cold on the cement porch. I thought, *Where's Mama? She should be here now.* I felt awkward, having a party with bunch of strangers all staring at me in a dress that was too stiff and way too big. Johnny told me earlier that I looked like the tooth he'd pulled out last week with a doorknob string. He had shown it me, all white and bloody. I socked him real hard when he said that. Mama looked down at me and said I'd grow into the dress soon after this birthday and that I had to put it on anyway because she had picked it out "special."

Standing up and smoothing out my big polka dot dress, I went back inside. I hollered out, "Mama, everyone's here. They're standing in the yard. What should I do?"

Waiting for her answer, I looked over at six packs of Coca-Cola and two rows of little pink nut cups. That room had a real good birthday feeling. I reached up sneakily and put my hand in one of the nut cups. "Mamaaaa." I didn't hear anything except my own teeth chewing. "Mmm, cashews and peanuts, my favorite." I took a few more and walked back to the bedroom. She wasn't there. Her dress was laid out all smooth on the bed, but she wasn't there. I peeked into the closet, wiped my salty hands on my polka-dot dress, and stepped out into the hall.

I walked into the bathroom, but I didn't see her at first. Then I saw a hand hanging over the edge of the tub. It was a tall tub so I had to walk right up to it. It was her ring hand. It was just dangling in the air. I guessed she was taking a bath, but I looked and there was no water in the tub. She was lying naked in a big pool of blood.

I grabbed her wrist and shook her arm. "Mama, Mama, wake up!" Her eyes stayed closed. "They're all here for the party. Johnny is givin' out the balloons. Wake up! Wake up!"

Her hand slid out of mine and dropped with a clink back into the tub. Climbing over the side, I tried not to step on her arm, but my dress was so big I couldn't see. I slipped on the blood and fell on top of her. Coming face-to-face with Mama, I started to cry. Shoving my puffy dress away from her face, I could see she was really hurt. Frantically, I wiped the blood off her arms and neck with big strokes, as the red and white polka dots on my dress blended together.

Jumping out of the tub, I ran to get help. "Johnny! Johnny! Mama's hurt! Mama's hurt!"

I pushed open the screen. There was so much noise and game playing on the clumpy lawn that no one even heard me come out. I screamed at the top of my lungs. "Somethin' is wrong with Mama! She won't wake up!"

Everyone's eyes turned toward me, and all the playing stopped. There were deep-throated gasps and even a few balloons got away. Shaking, I couldn't quite see their faces and didn't even feel the air. Then some mother rushed up to me while others went into the house. The only thing I felt were the hot tears streaming down my face, and I said over and over to anyone who'd listen, "Mama's hurt, Mama's hurt," until Johnny pulled me away.

It was only later that night when I was put to bed by the lady next door that I realized my new birthday red and white polka dot dress was completely soaked in blood. She babysat Johnny and me that night, and she told us that Mama was okay. Before we went to bed, Johnny snuck out. He overheard the mothers talking on the front porch. He said they said Mama had been drinking, slipped, fell, and cracked open the back of her head. She got twenty-something stitches and would be home in the morning. I wished Daddy had been there, but I also was glad he wasn't. One good thing came out of it, though. I got rid of that awful polka-dot birthday dress.

16

Very Cherry #9

Fall 1957

When I was five-and-a-half years old, I went to my first school. I was in kindergarten. I'd been going there for about three weeks, and my only friend was a little girl about my size. Nobody played with us, so we played together. We were both very shy, but it didn't matter that we didn't talk much. We just held hands and did everything together. She was my first friend besides Johnny. I don't remember her name, but I thought she was beautiful. Decades later I found our class picture, and there we were in the second row, holding hands. She was black, and I never even noticed.

Daddy had been gone a while, and we were living in a new apartment complex, Oneida Gardens. Johnny went to second grade at Concordia Lutheran. I went to Northridge Elementary up on the big hill way above Lake Washington.

One morning Mama made our lunches and went to work. I think it was work. Well, she went somewhere because Johnny walked me to the main road. He went straight on through the briar field to Concordia, and I went up the hill to kindergarten. It was a beautiful fall day, the kind of day where you could wear a sweater and knee socks with a little dress. I suddenly had to go to the bathroom really bad, and I didn't think I'd make it all the way to school. There was the busy street on one side of me and a wall with a hedge full of bushes on the other side. It was a very long twelve-block walk, and I was only about half way there. *I'll poop in my pants and walk real wide and go to the bathroom at school. No one will ever know,* I thought. I looked around, real secret like, and then I pooped hard and fast into my panties. As I walked the "wide" up the street carefully, my "Lincoln log" rolled out of Johnny's overstretched underwear and fell with a splat on the clean sidewalk.

All of a sudden, out of nowhere I heard "Eww, you pooped in your pants, you *pooped* in your pants! I'm going to tell the teacher. I'm going to tell the teacher." One of the cute boys in my kindergarten class pointed at the Lincoln log and ran around me and up the newly hosed sidewalk. I was devastated. There, for all to see, was a hard little brown log in the middle of the cement. Without looking, I dashed into the hedge and hid there for what seemed like forever.

No one was home, but I knew where the secret front-door key was hidden. I went back home, found the key, opened the side door to our apartment, and ate my lunch. Later, I changed my clothes and sat on the top stair of our back porch, with my legs tucked underneath me. I'd found one of Mama's lipsticks, her silver tubes. This one was called Very Cherry #9. I sat there, winding it up and down. I'm not really sure how it found its way into my little hand. Then I stood up and crossed toward the back door. Half of it was a window, and I saw my reflection and stopped. I looked at myself, stared, and then frowned.

"I'd better put on Mama's lipstick," I said importantly. I walked right up against the window pane and proceeded to draw lips on thinly, just like I remember Mama did. But I didn't like it, so I filled them in full so the outline reached all the way from my cheekbone to cheekbone. I was pleased, so pleased that I kissed the glass, and was surprised by my lip mark. I kissed it again and again and again till all the kisses wore out.

Full of the beauty of myself, and forgetting my earlier episode of the day, I turned away from the back door. On the mud hill where we played King of the Mountain, stood Albino Boy. I didn't know his real name. He was about five years old. Johnny always called him Albino. I thought he was really cute. I went down our three porch steps, out on the little walkway, and up and over to where the mud hill was. Sashaying, as Mama always called it, over to him, I said coyly, "Hi," puckering my mouth.

"What's that all over your face?" he said, his eyes squinting against the glaring sun.

"It's my Mama's Very Cherry #9," I said. "She had an extra one so she gave it to me. See?"

"Ugh," he said. "Looks like you been suckin' on somethin' that ain't dead yet."

"Oh." I squirmed. "That's awful! This is really rich and powerful color stuff," I said. "You put this on and, and ..." My mind was spinning. "You can fly!"

"Cannot," he said.

"Can so." I said.

"Cannot!" he shouted.

"Can too! Can too! You're just chicken. It's a magic tube, and you're just chicken." My eyes bore into his eyes hard. Finally, Albino Boy relented.

"Oh, yah?" he asked.

"Yah," I said. "You wanna try?"

"Well …" he started to say, but I cut him off.

"We gotta go to a secret place," I whispered. "Someplace where the bad evil won't see."

"Okay," he said after a long stare.

"I know. Let's go over behind the brick chimney."

Albino Boy turned, and I followed him. My mind was churning about what I would say next, but I'd started to believe that Very Cherry #9 had a magical power to make you fly. When Albino Boy and I reached the chimney, we checked to make sure no one was around. When we were finally sure, I took off the top and twisted it open. Looking at Albino Boy, I decided to start at the top of his head.

"I am goin' to put circles of red all over your flat top, so we can send signals to the fairy gods of magic flight that you're ready to fly."

His eyes bugged out, but he nodded his head. He stood firmly in the mud, ankle deep, and I climbed up a little higher on the rise so I could reach the top of his head. I tried paint circles, but they circles didn't seem to work. He couldn't fly. So I decided to do Indian markings. I continued on to his face, marking up his cheeks and nose and lips and ears, because I wanted to draw favorable spirits and fairies our way. That didn't help, so I convinced him to take off his shirt and sweater. I painted warrior circles around his nipples and his belly button and gave him facial markings on his tummy. But that didn't work either. He started to shake from the cold. I told him that if I inscribed the mummy's prayer on his bottom and painted his nunny, he would definitely rise up and go to heaven.

I was getting a little manic by this time. I was so excited. I helped him pull down his pants, but I was getting toward the end of the tube of Very Cherry. I painted his bottom, and as I came around and started to paint his nunny top, he started to cry. I stepped back off the mud mound and looked at him. All of a sudden I saw a very white boy with red circles on his head, nose and ears and markings on his chest, bottom, and nunny. He looked at me, let out a scream, and started to run away. I ran after him to give back his shirt, but he just ran faster and faster.

As I tripped over his pants, I heard him yelling, "I'm gonna tell my Mommy! I'm gonna tell my Mommy!" His voice faded.

I suddenly felt very alone standing in that mud and very naked. I picked up his sweater and trudged back to our back porch steps. I went back inside. I had a peanut butter and jelly sandwich and waited for Johnny to come home. Mama came home and wondered why I was there. I said I wasn't feeling so good so I came home.

Suddenly, from outside the back door, I heard a lady's voice screaming: "She's permanently stained my boy. He's pink. Pink!"

I ran into the bathroom and closed the door.

I heard my mother's voice. "Robin, get out here. Come here this minute."

I knew I was in for it. I put an Alka Seltzer on my tongue, just like Johnny had shown me, and I closed my mouth. I came out of the bathroom, looking very innocent and stood behind Mama's skirt. I couldn't believe what I saw. There was Albino Boy all red. Well, not red but pink. His hair was pink, his face was pink, his fingers were pink. I couldn't see his chest anymore because his mother had covered him up, but he was crying pink. His mother was screaming and pointing at me and pointing at Mama, who was now very angry. All the while I could feel the Alka Seltzer rising up in my mouth, just like the foaming dogs Johnny told me about.

Mama said, "Did you do this, Robin?" She tried not to choke on her fury.

I peeked out from behind her skirt, looking up at her and with all the dignity I could muster, I nodded yes. As I did, the foam started to spew out of my mouth and onto her skirt. It dripped on the floor. I had a great sense of power and strength. I was the god of volcano. They couldn't touch me.

17

❧

Flunking First Grade

Early Summer 1958

I don't know when I started to lip read, but it must have happened gradually. Maybe it was before Little Miss Jones; I don't know. What I do know is that I was in the first grade at Concordia Lutheran in Seattle for about two months when the nurse and the teacher realized I had hearing difficulties.

They said I must have lost my hearing gradually over the past few years, because my lip reading skills were pretty good. No one had really known. It did seem that Mama and everyone were yelling at me an awful lot. I didn't do things right or I wasn't where they wanted me to be. One day, just before the teacher noticed, Mama dropped the turkey pan behind me, and I didn't even flinch. It was then that she realized that I wasn't just stupid. Maybe that picture of me with my mouth wide open in front of the Memphis zoo way back in 1955 was the beginning of it; for some reason I thought if I kept my mouth open, my third ear would hear more. Or maybe

87

it started even when I was just a one-year-old, with my head just laying there and poaching in my juice.

It's kind of funny to think that I flunked first grade. Who flunks first grade? But I went from Concordia Lutheran to a special school on Capitol Hill for children who are hard of hearing. We were really poor. Daddy was in jail someplace for driving drunk, so very little money came in. Mama was working at a building with a globe on top, and three times a week we would go with her and stay at this daycare center while she worked. She did something at the paper. That's what she called it, the paper with the spinning world on top. Three times a week, early in the morning she drove in and parked, and we saw the world spinning on top of her building.

"Where does your mommy work?" she'd ask, all dressed up with lipstick.

"At the world, the spinnin' world!" we'd say and point. She'd park in the open lot, and we'd walk over to the tall building across the street. It was brown brick and had what seemed to be a million floors. We'd enter through the glass doors and take the elevator up to the third floor, which was a daycare for mothers who worked downtown. I didn't like it much. I felt like I was inside a cocoon, and I was very alone, even with Johnny there. I had trouble understanding people, so I just stayed shy.

The ABC room was brown and stank. The only time I felt comfortable was when I was out on the rooftop playground all by myself. It was usually very cold and rainy, but I loved going out there. I felt free. The beans and franks on Wednesdays were good too. They were my favorite. I used to save all the wiener cuts for the end, and

I would nibble them all around the edges until they were almost gone. It took me a long time to eat my beans and franks. We had nap time on green cots that smelled of hand soap and dried urine. I was a green-cot bed-wetter too.

Somehow, Johnny managed to slip out of the ABC room many times. He even set fire in three elevators. When Mama came over in fury, he said he didn't like the way the carpet smelled. She was really angry, especially since she would lose a whole day's pay and maybe lose her job. After that, we had only oatmeal for the whole week, three times a day. I pretended to cry and watched Johnny tie his shoelaces together as we left the building. Secretly I grinned inside because I loved oatmeal, and I really didn't like that place, except for the wieners and beans.

For about six months I went to the hearing school with the funny ear hats, and then we flew to Georgia, where my uncle took my adenoids out. I'd had my tonsils out earlier, but they grew back in funny. At the hearing school I took little yellow pills to shrink the scar tissue. I took those pills for almost two years.

I can still remember the skinny lady with the pointy stick who made us mouth the words on the chalkboard. By then I was somewhere inside myself, and the only time I paid any real attention to Mama was when she put her face in front of mine. I really didn't hear anything but my own thoughts, and they seemed to be much nicer than being poked or prodded. Most people thought I was just not paying attention. But they didn't understand; I couldn't hear them. What was especially wonderful was that I couldn't hear Johnny's awful air rifle anymore.

Later that spring, I started first grade again, this time in Columbus, Georgia. I think I only went to that first grade for a couple of months. It was very different from the school in Seattle. Everything was separate there; they put people in different places. Brown people had to go through different doors and drink from faraway fountains. In this school, everyone was white. It wasn't like kindergarten in Seattle,, where my best friend had been black. She was my only friend.. This school was very different and had segregation laws. It was very white, with lots of church columns and a playground full of teeter-totters.

While I was in this second first grade, Nanny Munn gave me an emerald ring for my birthday. I was watching the teacher and thought I would clean my ring; so I took it off my finger and stuck it in my mouth and sucked. But I sucked so hard, I swallowed it, way down to the place where you can't feel it anymore. I knew I was going to get in trouble and, sure enough, I did. Mama made me go out and get a big long switch. After she spanked me over the tub, she told me to tell her whenever I took a poop. I didn't know why until I saw this big stick near the toilet. About two weeks went by, and every time I took a poop, Mama took that big, old, dried-up stick and stabbed at my poop balls, looking for that ring. But I held my breath real hard, trying to keep it inside me. I could just see it, like a cartoon, hanging off one of the tips of my ribs.

That was my second first grade. I still didn't communicating very well with other children, and I was pretty shy. I guess that little, tiny yellow tissue-shrinking pill worked, because by fall I could hear a little bit more. But it wasn't until third grade that my inner-ear tissue shrank down, and I could fully understand people again.

18

❦

Seaweed on the Train Tracks

Spring 1960

A few plastic Easter eggs were still scattered around the duplex when Mama came home from the hospital. In the white blanket bundled in her arms was my new brother Darren. After Mama settled him in his crib, she invited me to see him. The first time I met him was under a rainbow arch of his urine. His nunny was standing straight up as Mama tried to change his diaper. Johnny whacked at the rainbow bears over his head as Mama closed the duck pins. "Stop that, Johnny," she whispered as she tried to keep the baby quiet.

Then Daddy walked in. He and Mama hadn't been getting along at all lately, especially in the months before Darren was born. They spat out words I couldn't quite understand in low tones. Johnny saved the day. "Daddy, can me and Sis go for a ride in your new car?" he said as he pulled on Daddy's sleeve.

Mama said, "That's a good idea, Tiny. Why don't you take them for a ride?"

Daddy nodded okay, and he lifted me up into his arms. Johnny grabbed our jackets, and we went out the front door.

Daddy had a beautiful shiny black Ford with a V back. He was very proud of it. Heading west, he drove us down to the Golden Gardens Beach and south to the Tide Water restaurant, near the train bridge over the locks. Daddy said he was going in for awhile and told us to go and play on the beach. I knew he was upset for some reason. He had that drinking look on his face. More than likely, he would be at the bar.

It was a typical rainy Seattle day, early afternoon before the fog rolled in. Seagulls squawked overhead. Washed-up kelp and rotting baby crab legs were strewn across the sand. Johnny found a glass fish buoy under some driftwood. I liked watching the sand fleas jump as I prodded the bulbous kelp heads with my toe. Before we knew it, Johnny and I had walked way down the beach. The bar was almost around the curve, almost out of sight. It must have been a weekday because there weren't many people around.

Johnny and I saw four boys coming toward us. They were skipping rocks across the waves and fake-fighting with each other. I wasn't paying much attention because I was looking at a ferry cutting north up the Sound.

When I did look up, the older boys were almost on top of us. They threw rocks at Johnny and me and asked for money. Johnny said we didn't have any, took my hand, and turned back toward the restaurant. We did our fast walk, but the wet sand slowed our pace. The big boys got around in front of us, perhaps because their shoes were bigger.

One of them clutched me by the arm and started to drag me up toward the road. Johnny followed, yelling and tugging on one of their parkas. "Let her go; let my sister go." The two larger boys grabbed Johnny from behind. One even covered his mouth and proceeded to force him behind me. I think they were around thirteen because they had big red pimples and dark, fuzzy hair on their upper lips. They were twice Johnny's size and three times my size. Johnny and I tried to fight them off as we went up the sand dune, but by the time we got to the street, they had a really good hold on us.

When the traffic died down, they ran us across the two-lane road to the bottom of a gully. There were train tracks way above us on the top of a bushy hill covered with wet ferns and broken trees. The boys pushed me up the side of the hill, even though I kept sliding and getting stuck in the dirt and mud. Johnny also fought all the way. One of the boys grabbed some long kelp and seaweed and carried it up the hill with him. We didn't see it until we were up by the train tracks.

When we got up to the top, we could see that down a bit, there was a little train house with a big arm extended out over the railroad tracks. The boys used the S-word and the F-word a lot; one of them even smoked. A tall boy with really bad whitehead acne grabbed me by the arm and said, "I'm gonna tie you to the railroad tracks unless you gimme some money."

I said, choking, "I don't have any money, I don't have any—"

Johnny interrupted angrily, "Let her go. She's only in the … in the … first grade. Let her go! My Daddy's a big important cop, a detective! And he's going to get you."

My mouth dropped open because I knew Johnny was fibbing. I was in the third grade, and Daddy was a traveling salesman. Johnny looked at me real hard, nodding his head yes, so I bit my lip and didn't say anything. I was scared, real scared, and I knew Johnny was too.

As we stood there, the short, stocky boy punched Johnny in the stomach a couple of times while the cigarette-sucking boy picked his pockets. They took out all his change and his favorite whistle, the chrome one Papa Munn had given him the previous Christmas.

The tall boy with the whitehead acne yanked me over to the train tracks and onto the wood ties. We walked down about twelve ties until we were just past the little train house. I tried to squirm and wiggle out of my jacket. I could hear Johnny hollering the S-word at the tall kid way back behind me.

When we finally stopped, the tall boy hooked me using his arms, tripped me, and laid me down on the tracks. I kept kicking and fighting him, but it didn't do me any good. He was just too strong. The quiet boy who was carrying the kelp came up casually beside him and stepped over me. Dropping the seaweed, he bent down and proceeded to tie up my ankles with the long slick kelp. The tall boy kept his knee on my chest and with both hands he held my arms over my head until my feet were tight and secure. I tried to scream, but the older acne boy stuffed the edge of his open parka in my mouth. I could taste the metal zipper as I felt the rocks piercing through the legs of my thin cotton pants. My ankle bones knocked together when I tried to kick free from the kelp. I was really knotted up good. The boys tied up my wrists over the cold, damp, rail. Warm tears rolled out the sides of my eyes and flowed back into my eyes. I tried to shake off the continuous stream of wet tears as I listened to Johnny's heels scuffling in the rocks while the two other boys laughed and held him back.

From somewhere in the distance, I heard the faint sound of a train whistle coming from the locks. Johnny burst out with, "My dad's a police officer! He has a special black car, and he's looking for us now! See?" He pointed down through the bushes toward a car that looked just like Daddy's. "It's the detective's car from the downtown precinct!"

The older boys didn't seem to be at all scared by Johnny's threats. Instead, the two boys holding Johnny made him smoke a cigarette while the other two finished knotting me to the tracks. After a while, the two boys dragged Johnny over to where I was tied, and all four of them taunted him: "You better give us all your money, stupid." "We're gonna kill you sister." From where my head was, I knew that a train was getting closer. I wasn't sure if I heard it or it was because of the funny sensation on the back of my head from the metal rail, which was starting to buzz.

Again Johnny pointed down to the road and said with fear rising in his voice, "There he goes again. Our dad's looking for us. He's the chief of police! He's gonna find you and put you all in jail!"

Then, perhaps because I prayed really hard, the gray heavens opened up, and walnut-sized pellets of rain splashed down on my face and bounced off the railroad tracks. It was Seattle at its very best; we had rain, hard, spitting, cold, chilling rain. The tall whitehead acne boy whined and whimpered. "Aw, let's get outta here. They're just two little shitheads and we only got thirty-five cents. We're not getting anymore."

The other boys agreed, nodding and zipping up their jackets. The acne boy gave me one good kick to the ribs, and within seconds all four disappeared into the bushes. I heard them slipping and sliding on their butts all the way down the muddy hill.

Johnny ran over to me. I could hear the train getting closer and closer. It must have been just on the Ballard side of the locks. Johnny and I struggled with my wrist knots, but the rain made the kelp very slippery. When I pulled, they got tighter and Johnny's wet fingers couldn't untie them. Johnny looked around for something sharp to cut the seaweed with. I could hear the train starting to thunder the rail on the tracks. I was getting a sick feeling in my stomach; it was raining so hard, I knew the train man wouldn't be able to see me.

Johnny finally found a sharp piece of broken brick, and he began to cut on the underside of the knot. He slashed and slashed at the seaweed until the kelp tore open, and I was free on both ends. Quickly, he lifted me up and I stepped over the now vibrating rail and over to the mud side of the tracks. Within seconds, the train's grill came into view. Stepping back into the bushes about three feet from the train tracks, Johnny and I froze and watched as the huge noisy train whooshed by on the wet train tracks: ka-thump, ka-thump, ka-thump. We had just made it. One minute I faced decapitation, and the next, I realized I had an okay older brother. I was so proud of Johnny. He was so brave. I'll never forget that. He saved me. My big brother saved me.

Cautiously, Johnny looked down the muddy embankment to see if the boys were still there, but it was raining so hard he couldn't tell. He decided it would be best to walk back along the railroad tracks until we were just above the Tidewater restaurant. Then it would be safe to slide down the embankment, cross the road, and find Daddy. Hand in hand in the pouring rain, Johnny and I walked along next to the rails. We were soaked, but we didn't care. I was floating. I had the biggest, bravest brother in the whole wide world. What a day: a new baby brother, a near-death experience, and a new hero.

19

Wenatchee Car Crash

Summer 1961

It was late, the kind of late when your tummy is starting to think about breakfast. Daddy drove like the car was dancing. He kept swerving way left and then way right, almost kissing other car bumpers. Darren, my new baby brother, was in the front seat, sandwiched between Mama and Daddy. Tallulah the Second headed east, toward Wenatchee. We had just left my Daddy's sister's apple orchards. You could almost smell the morning coming up, that dreamy dark time before the peek-a-boo light.

I wanted to take control, but I couldn't reach the wheel from where I was sitting. So I pressed my face to my window. I could see and hear everything so clearly: the stars, the trees, and the Wenatchee River rushing by. I looked at the guard rail, which teased like a loose ribbon. The speeding lights on the two-lane highway kept coming and going, white and then red. But everything inside our car, especially in the back seat, made me feel nervous.

Suddenly, our right front headlight connected with

the guard rail. There were screeching noises and glass went flying. I reached across the back of the middle seat and grabbed Darren's head. There were shouts and screams, all skidding together; then all of a sudden we were heading in the other direction with our car sliding down the railing.

When I came to, I realized we had done a complete circle and were balanced over an abyss where we could hear the rushing water beneath us. Everything got quiet. Johnny jumped over me, opened the side door, and was gone. I saw that Darren was all right between Mama and Daddy, who were off in some taffy world, drunk and yelling and screaming at each other.

I followed Johnny outside the car and started to run. I ran up the road. I ran and ran. I could hear the gravel beneath my feet. I saw all these cars going by, and I saw all these distorted faces and tree-frog fingers on the car windows looking back at me. I couldn't understand why I couldn't see as clearly as I just had inside my own car. I ran and ran. Cars were screeching and stopping ,and I just knew I had to get away.

I thought Johnny had gone down where the rushing water was. I didn't know for sure until days later that he had literally run into the apple orchards and the woods for three days.

As I ran up the road I saw an old gas station that had been shut down. There was no one around. I went and hid behind a pump. I don't know how long I was there, but a man in a brown hat, a police officer, came by. He put his flashlight on me and tried to talk to me, but I was scared. I didn't want to be where grownups were. We played tag around the pumps. I out maneuvered him a couple of times, but he finally caught me and put me in the patrol car. He drove me back up the hill to my aunt's house and apple orchards.

The day before, when we were having pickles my aunt had made, I asked, "Where are the pickle trees?" She told me how stupid I was, that pickles don't grow on trees, they grow on the ground.

The patrolman took me back to the house. When I got there, Johnny couldn't be found, and Daddy had evidently been locked up for drunken driving, but Mama was there and Darren was back at my aunt's house. She had bruises on her cheeks and hands, but she acted quite normal. She took me into the bathroom after the policeman left. There, she whipped me with a belt, as she cried and told me how much I embarrassed her. She still stank of booze. Then she dragged me out to a shed, where the potatoes and apples were, out by the old outhouse. She locked me in. It wasn't a cold night, but the apples were cool around me. I built a little house around my feet and legs and drifted off to sleep.

Next thing I knew, light came in through split beams on the shack siding. I saw clearly that I was in there with potatoes and apple stacks and baskets, somewhere near the floor. Someone was shaking the door and working at the lock. It opened, and light flooded in. I heard Daddy's voice, but I couldn't see him.

He said, "Are you all right, Robin?"

I said, "I'm fine Daddy," hoping that he wasn't still drunk.

He said, "Now you come outta there. I talked to your

Mom. Everything's all right. And guess what? I gotta surprise for ya."

I was too stiff and cold to reply. I stood up and walked toward his dark shadow. His rough hands picked me up and into the light. He didn't seem to be drunk anymore. As he held me, he gave me a wooden Pinocchio doll.

"It's very nice, Daddy," I said.

He said, "It's a magic wishin' doll. One of the ladies in Leavenworth Village was makin' these wooden dolls, and I thought you'd might like to have one."

"Yes, Daddy," I said, squinting. The sun felt good on my back and head. I hadn't realized how cold I was. We stayed at my aunt's house for another two days. The same policeman brought Johnny back, and he also got a whipping. Mama always did the whipping, but she didn't lock him in the shack.

The next time we left at daylight. We drove back through Wenatchee but this time Mama and Daddy weren't drunk. We were on the road again, heading east. Off to another destination. Now I had two dolls to dress and hide, Mr. Navy and my long-nosed Pinocchio.

20

"Peacock Lady" Dance School

Fall 1961

My first introduction to "the dance" came after St. Patrick's Day. I was a very plump, shy thumb-sucker. Johnny, Mama, Darren and I were living back in Oneida Gardens, where four years earlier I had initiated Albino Boy with Very Cherry #9.

Mama worked fulltime at the *Post Intelligencer* in the classified section. All the while she was slyly husband hunting. I'm not sure where she got the money for Loretta Anderson's School of Dance, but I got to study there for four months.

Miss Anderson was the beautiful "Peacock Lady" from the Ziegfeld Follies. There were pictures of her all over the dance studio, and a couple of those plumes hung over the entrance to the dance room. To get to dance class on Saturday was a bit of a walk from Oneida Gardens, but it was only half as far from Concordia Lutheran, and I went on Wednesdays after school.

I remember how rich I felt when Mama and I went to

the dance store and bought my first pink ballet slippers. I'm sure I tied them up all wrong, but they made me feel so pretty with big pink bows hanging down. We didn't have enough money for me to carry them in a nice bag like some of the rich girls did, with their sparkly snaps and pretty ballerinas painted on the outside. So I kept mine in my lunch sack. I walked all the way down Thirty-fifth Street, almost to the bridge, to take my two weekly lessons. On Saturday, Miss Anderson let me take as many classes as I wanted but only charged Mama for two.

Inside the first room, there was the office desk and sign-in sheet. There were always lots of mothers and sweaty girls there. There was one big change room where the girls could get dressed; the boys used the bathroom because there weren't very many boys. The first room had pictures of Miss Anderson with her plumes, beautiful ladies with fancy costumes, and black-and-white prints of stiff ballerinas. Once we went through the narrow glass doors, we were in the studio.

Three thick pillars separated the ballet bar from the mirrors. All over the floor were little squares of dirty beige linoleum; the edges were kind of peeled up on the sides. We had to be careful when doing leaps across the floor to make sure we didn't trip on one of the big flaps of linoleum. There was also a box in which the big girls with hard box shoes stuck their toes. There was a special box with old box shoes that the big girls had thrown away near the front desk. The dance school didn't have a pianist; it didn't even have a piano, just an old, scratchy, two-speaker record player.

I had a wonderful time there. When I took ballet

class, I always used the second bar. Only the big girls could put their leg on the top bar. It smelled of sweat and rosin and little girls' wet hair. In jazz class, we learned dance moves with animal names, like the grasshopper, in which we bent one front leg and hopped out long on the back leg. To do the frog, which I was pretty good at, I squatted with the weight on my hands and hopped across the floor. Miss Anderson said I made a great toad. I wasn't sure if that was a compliment or not.

Then there was the butterfly. It looked better on the tall girls because they could get their arms flapping and really speed across the floor. I especially liked the dragonfly, because we got to flap, jump, stretch out long, and buzz around the room. Once I got going, it was pretty hard to stop. I sure did like to dance. Years later at Cornish School of Allied Arts in Seattle when I studied ballet with Miss Irving, I was amazed that there were French words for a lot of those animal dance moves.

Miss Anderson's daughter, Miriam, was beautiful. She had big breasts and the prettiest dark chocolate hair I ever saw. She had long, thick lashes with just a hint of charcoal on the edges. I think she was up for "Miss America" or "Miss Washington Apple" or something like that. She was gone the whole summer from dance classes, and I never saw her again. I think I heard Mama say that she was making babies.

Miss Anderson took a real liking to me because I was pretty coordinated. I wasn't shy in class like I was in school. I'd jump, turn, and do anything she'd ask me to do. I only took classes there about four months, until the end of the summer, and then Mom couldn't pay anymore. Those were the oatmeal days.

I'll never forget one Saturday after July 4. After jazz class, Miss Anderson said, "Robin, go find yourself a used pair of pointy shoes in the box near my desk. Open my second drawer and bring me the box of lambs' wool too. Now shut your mouth, and go find a pair that fit." I couldn't believe it. This was going to be my first pointe class. I was one of the big girls now. I found a pair that fit pretty well. Slipping into the hard box shoes, I lifted the heel up over my socks. Waddling noisily and dragging the dirty ribbons behind me, I walked back into the prestigious class. I know now that it was a very incorrect way of learning pointe, but at that time I was ecstatic.

Dance was my first introduction to the arts. I probably wouldn't have ever gone there if I hadn't been kicked out of Campfire Girls; then my Brownie troop moved away and never gave Mama a forwarding address. I didn't like the Brownies anyway. They always had lousy treats, and their furniture was covered in clear plastic.

The dance school was one of my first creative outlets. I am so grateful for the few months I spent there. It wasn't until a few years later that I had the same artistic feeling. I found track and field, ran dashes, and was pretty good. All through Blaine Junior High, Queen Anne High School, and then eventually musical theater at United States International University School of Performing Arts, I realized how important Miss Anderson's dance classes were to me.

I'll always remember my first dance recital. I was a chubby nine-year-old doing the Peppermint Twist with a little boy next to me on my right. I was too fat for my Charleston costume so my back zipper slid all the way down. Keeping as much to Miss Anderson's choreography as I could, I squeezed my arms in tight, making little circles in front of my chest. My dancing partner's pants were too big, and they slid down to around his knees. Standing there in his underwear and seeing me shaking my fringe, he started to scream. Miss Loretta had to run out from the wings, pick him up, and carry him off the stage. All the while, I never lost a twisting beat. The audience broke into applause, hoots, and laughter. I stayed on stage until the bitter Peppermint Twist ended. It was my first solo bow. Even though I spent most of the time trying not to fall out of my costume, that moment really hooked me.

21

Concordia Lutheran
and Early Puberty

Fall 1962

I was ten years old. Mama was looking for a new husband.
Johnny and I were enrolled at the nearby Concordia
Lutheran Elementary School. It was a long flat, white,
two-story building with an asphalt playground that led
to a thorny nettle grove. A portable building housed the
third and fourth grades. That's the room I was in. During
school races and teen fair exhibits, we wore felt blue-and-
white beanies with a big red C on them for Concordia.
The Catholic school had uniforms; we had beanies.

I was a little distraught because Daddy wasn't around
much. In memory of him, I did a lot of his morning
bathroom routine. I don't know how long this went on,
but in the morning, when I went to the bathroom, I made
all the sounds he used to make. I'd grunt, I'd bear down,
I'd make wheezing, choking Fred Flintstone noises that

I remembered coming from behind the smoky bathroom door.

One day at school I was going to the girl's lavatory in the basement. The third–and–fourth–grade building was on the playground and didn't have a bathroom. I got permission from Miss Schullenberger, and I went into the main building to go to the bathroom. After I wiped and turned around to flush, I saw that the pee in the bowl was all red. I thought, *Oh my God, I'm dyin'.* I flushed long, pulled up my panties, and ran quickly upstairs into the nurse's office.

The nurse said, "Robin, Robin, what's wrong?" I can't remember her name, but I told her I had just seen a lot of blood in the toilet bowl. I'll never forget that knowing smile on her face. She looked down at me all white and stiff, and said, "Well, you're a bit small and a little young, but maybe it's time." Then she took me into the second room, the "when you're really sick" room. It was where we got shots and lay down when we fainted in the hall. She took out this little thing and unwrapped it. It looked like a big elastic rubber–band with two little hooks. *A strange contraption*, I thought. Then she brought out this huge white tissue box and pulled out a white log. She had me take my panties off, and she showed me how to hook the tips of the white tissue log onto this elastic belt and then step through it and pull it up. It hung right between my plump little thighs. It felt very odd, like I had pooped a log, and it had dried hard. Anyway, I pulled up my panties up over it, but it stuck out like a dog's nose from underneath the front of my skirt and way out the back. I looked like an A-frame sideways from my waist down. I was embarrassed.

The nurse sat me down, smiled, and said, "This happens to all young ladies." Then she gave me a book. "Tell your mother what wonderful miracle happened to you today and have her go over the book with you, especially the bathing section. She gave my shoulders a squeeze and led me into the first office room. "Now go on back to class and mark this day on your calendar." With that the nurse closed the first office door, and I was out in the hall.

I looked down at the flimsy book. On the cover was a picture of a beautiful, blonde girl, kind of like Cinderella with little daisies and flowers all around her. The book's title was *The Miracle and Joys of Becoming a WOMAN*. The nurse told me to wear the pad and change to a fresh one the next day. Thank goodness she gave me a couple more logs in a paper bag. I could just hear the other kids razzing me. I started to slink my way across the hall and down the stairs. I checked to make sure nobody was looking. I kept my back up against the wall try to push the dog's nose back between my legs. I felt like a duck. I was going to waddle and everybody would know I was wearing this miracle of womanhood. I never told Mama, and I never changed the log. I slept with it for three days and wore double underwear so that it wouldn't bend out. I hid it when I took a bath and put it back in when I went to bed. I didn't bleed again that I remember.

Four days later the nurse stopped me in the hall and said, "So Robin, how are you doing? Did you change your pad?"

I shook my head and whispered, "No, I didn't, ma'am."

The nurse jerked her head back and said, "You haven't changed your pad?" Her face flushed, and she looked hot. Then she took me sternly by the left arm and dragged me into her office and plopped me down. "Now Robin, tell me. Why haven't you changed your pad? I gave you fresh ones."

"Well, I don't need one, ma'am," I replied meekly. "My pee-pee bowl water hasn't been red, and I'm not leaking anymore."

"Tell me, Robin," the nurse prodded, sitting on the edge of her steel desk. "What are your bathroom habits?"

"Huh?"

"I mean," the nurse said, "how do you go to the bathroom?"

I squirmed in my chair. "Well, I go to the bathroom like my Daddy does."

She raised her painted eyebrows. "And how's that?"

I said very proudly with my chest up high while sitting tall in the metal chair, my feet dangling. "I sit on the potty and then I go grrriyah, until I'm done."

She sat back, rocked and laughed, trying to hold herself in. I never thought a nurse could laugh like that. I couldn't understand what she thought was so funny. After wiping her eyes, she said, "Robin, you haven't started your menstrual cycle. You've been straining."

She took my hand, and we both walked back to the special sick room. After she closed the door, I stepped out of my undies. With her help, I unhooked the bent white log, which by now was rubbed raw all along the edges. The nice nurse showed me how to roll up the pad and discard it. After washing my hands in the high sink, the usually strict nurse gave me a long hug. I walked out the two doors and back into the hall. Thank goodness it was recess time because all my friends were outside.

I didn't strain again for a long, long time. The real thing happened about three years later.

22

Melted Chocolate and the Last Fight

Spring 1963

I called Daddy at the glass-blowing place where he worked. There, they cut glass and mirrors to replace broken ones in houses and big stores. I asked him if he wanted to come over that night. Mama had a date, so I made him promise that he would leave before she got back. He said he couldn't wait to see me. It would just be Johnny, baby Darren (who was a little over a year old), and me in our Oneida Gardens top-floor, two-bedroom apartment. We moved there when Mama started bringing all our prospective new fathers home.

I was so excited that Daddy was coming over. I hadn't seen him in three long months. He arrived a little after eight when it was all clear. I let him in, and he swooped me up in his arms and gave me a big kiss. He didn't smell like bourbon either. I was so glad. He took a paper sack into the kitchen and told me to stay where I was. I yelled from the sofa that Johnny was playing with the big boys in the caves below the housing project. I told him about how they planned wars, stole graham crackers, and lit candles down where the old shovel scoops left water under the main apartment building. Daddy didn't answer me back so I guessed it was all fine.

Darren was sound asleep. I let Daddy tiptoe in and peek in on him. "He's a good baby," I whispered. "Doesn't cry much. I take care of him when Mama's gone." I was glad I had Daddy all to myself. He brought me our special favorite sharing thing. It was one of those big almond Hershey bars that we ate in our own special way.

We went back to the living room and sat on the couch. His big, smoke-smelling arm wrapped all around me. We watched that funny show Dick Van Dyke show. I loved the way he could fall over furniture. Daddy brushed my shoulder-length hair as I sat between his knees. He never caught my ears the way Mama did. As we watched, we licked big chunks of the almond Hershey. He hadn't hurt me since our last trip, so I wasn't scared that way. I didn't mind that he was drinking now, because he was going to leave soon. He had promised. I missed him so much when he was gone. Why didn't Mama like him? She was different now, getting all gussied up and perfumed, and wearing real high, pretty, pointed shoes. But she was beautiful and seemed a lot happier without Daddy around.

The Cordovas, who lived across the hall from us, had one boy named Chris. He was Johnny's age. The week before Chris and I sat on the back porch steps with a medical encyclopedia. It had lots of pictures. Chris was looking up breasts and asked me to point out what breast size I was. "Was that okay, Daddy?" I asked. "He didn't touch me the way you do."

Daddy didn't say anything for a long time. He just pulled tight down on my hair, took a sip, went into the kitchen, and poured another. I had three more pieces of square chocolate before he returned. "Robin," he said. "Don't you ever, ever let anyone touch you the way Daddy does. It's special and just between you and me." Sucking on my fingers, I nodded and turned back toward the TV. I could feel him pacing back and forth behind me. Getting comfortable back on the couch, I chocolate-drooled myself off to sleep.

The next thing I knew, I woke up to Mama and Daddy arguing in the little dining room off the kitchen. *What is Daddy still doing here? I'm going to get it.* Mama was mad, and it felt late. They must have been arguing for a long while because Mama's coat was off and so were her shoes. I guess I'd really been sound asleep. I knew Johnny was home because he had slammed the bathroom door and was yelling, "Stop it! Stop it!" I could hear Darren starting to wake up and cry from our room.

Mama went into the kitchen and returned with a heavy cast-iron skillet, the one we made hamburgers in. Daddy slapped her hard after something she said, and she threatened him with the pan. Daddy went for her throat, but she hauled off and hit him a couple times in the head. His glasses broke and blood came out of his cheek and nose. As Daddy grabbed Mama, she dropped the pan. That was the last thing I heard. They struggled and fought, knocking over the dining room chairs. As

Mama lay on the floor, Daddy picked her up by the back of the neck, grabbed her around the waist, and turned her upside down. He shook her like an upside-down sack of potatoes, banging her head over and over on top of the floor. Blood came out everywhere. I yelled, but I couldn't hear my own words.

I pushed myself up into the corner next to the TV. If I could have pushed myself through the wall, I would have. I had the sensation that my whole body was trying to scream out of my mouth to stop them. Then there was pounding coming from somewhere, but I didn't know where. I heard fists on the front door, and people yelling from somewhere outside.

Finally the door broke open like a big splinter, and two policemen came in, followed by the Cordovas from next door. There was a whirlwind of grabbing and handcuffs and towels, and then Mama and Daddy were gone. Johnny crept out of the bathroom to watch the end of the fight. As the sounds started to filter back in, I realized that my ears were ringing. I still couldn't talk. It was as if someone had taken my words and shoved them back down inside me with no way out.

When all the commotion stopped, Johnny said, "You're gonna get it."

Mrs. Cordova came back in and told us that they had taken Daddy away and that Mama was at the hospital getting fixed up. As she walked into the kitchen to get a bottle of milk for Darren, she saw the blood dripping down the dining room walls. "Jesus, Mary of God!" she said, crossing herself, and then went into the bathroom instead.

I don't remember what happened for a long time after that. I know I never called Daddy again or had him come over. Johnny and I also started to treat Mama's dates a little better. That was the first time it really hit me that my parents were never going be together again.

23

Prospective Fathers

Summer 1964

Mama was working hard at the newspaper job and trying to take care of us three kids by herself. Darren was around one or two. I was in my dance-school years, and Johnny was getting up to no good.

Mama started to search for a money-rolled, nice-looking man who wanted to join our family and support her snot-runny kids. It was a hard thing back then, I'm sure. But Mama was a looker, so I knew she'd eventually find a good, handsome man. Different types of men came over to our apartment in Oneida Gardens. Johnny and I were pretty tough on them. If we didn't like them, we broke the toys that they gave us when their backs were turned. We picked out the turquoise stones on the watchbands or lost the dice and cards from the board games. Darren didn't know what was going on; he was just a gurgling, bottle-sucking runt of a kid.

Mama was flirting and highfaluting with all of them, but we could tell the ones she really liked. They made

it through the apartment door. Then they had to endure
the torture Johnny and I heaped on them. If I didn't like
them, I'd bring out Mama's special teeth glass from the
bathroom and say, "You know what Mama does with
her teeth at night? She soaks them." I was still a thumb-
sucking kid, but all in all I knew which one was going to
be the right kind of Dad for us.

Sometimes we peeked out of our second-floor window
and watched her kissing them on the downstairs porch.
Some were short and fat; others had moustaches. Mama
would let them leave with just a handshake, but she'd still
bring in the candy and flowers.

There was this special guy. We didn't see him for a
long time. He had a little red bug hump of a car. I later
learned it was called a Karmann Ghia. This special man
of Mama's was tiny, a lot smaller than my real father. He
and Mama used to stay out late, long after we were in
bed. I guess they talked in the car. We never saw them
smooching, but I couldn't really see into that bug hump
car because the windows were way too small.

Boy oh boy, Johnny and I tortured all those other
men. I remember this big Texan. His stomach kind of
hung over his belt, and he wore a cowboy vest with
fringe. He's the one who gave us the watches with the
turquoise stones. He also gave me some sweater clips with
blue stones in silver, which I picked out with a cinnamon
toothpick when he left and hid them in a special memory
box. The Texan's breath smelled of burnt cigars, and
Johnny and I decided that he just wasn't right. Mama
said he had a lot of money and that we'd probably have

to move to Texas, Armadillo or something like that. I'm sure glad we didn't.

There were a couple of squirrelly type men, too. One was even an athletic coach at some high school in Renton. I knew he was going to give Johnny a hard time, so I did some stuff to his muffler with a potato, and Johnny tried to slash his tire with his pocketknife. It wasn't sharp enough, so we hoped when he drove away that the potato would do the trick. We never saw him again; it must have worked.

24

The Fort Lawton Dance Recital

Early Winter 1964

From somewhere Mama found the money to pay Loretta Anderson for one month of dance classes. Two weeks before Christmas, we did a special holiday recital at the Fort Lawton Army Base in Magnolia, a suburb of Seattle.

I was involved in one number, the finale. My dancing specialty was turns. I was to twirl on in a half-moon circle doing pique turns or flamingo turns, as Miss Anderson called them. I was the exciting month of December that united the other eleven months for the lengthy closing bow.

This special performance took place outside the mess hall in a huge recreation room with an open dance floor at one end. There were flags and army stuff everywhere. In the hallway lobby I stood in my Gerber-yellow-squash-colored, three-quarter-length net tutu (with my brother's shoestrings for shoulder straps), feeling naked and ugly. All the other girls had mamas fussing over them, fixing them up with sparkles and ribbons and hairspray. I had gotten my ballet shoes from the used shoe box. Since I had only taken four months of lessons, Mama didn't want to buy me a new pair. That was okay by me; someplace inside me, I think I understood. All the rich kids at the studio had new, colored shoes, car rides, and fancy trimming on their costumes.

I felt ugly and lonely. One of the soloists was practicing her performance in the hallway, and I got the idea to go out to the car and have some of Mama's special water juice that was hidden under the front seat. I knew it would give me a fuzzy, funny feeling and make me not feel less sad. I took three or four big guzzles. I laughed and suddenly felt brave.

Walking back into the hallway I saw a big Christmas tree, all lit and decorated, at the end of the room. It occurred to me that my costume for the December solo should have been white, red, or green. But no, I had Gerber yellow, a Thanksgiving color, the perfect color for August and corn. Since we didn't pay for the costume, I got the squash-colored one that nobody wanted was mine. I had thought November, a girl with glasses, might want that color; but no, she took the white one. February, a girl with two left feet, took the red; and mousy May took the emerald-green one because her mother drove a rich Cadillac.

Those girls had their mothers sew sequins around their elastic bodices, and some had big fluffs of marabou feathers laced around their hems. April had a big blue bow and sparkly silver ribbons. Mousy May wore the biggest tiara I'd ever seen, and all the girls had on nice, new pink tights. We couldn't afford any tights, and there were none in the "throw out" box. If I was to represent the best month of the year, why couldn't I have a pretty costume and stretchy new tights like everybody else? I was pissed.

I was also upset because I hadn't seen Daddy in a while. Mama and Daddy hadn't seen each other since the big Hershey fight. I called his office, told him about the recital, and suggested that maybe he could sneak in the back. I hadn't heard anything, so I didn't know if he would show up. It was just as well because I was really embarrassed about my costume.

Miss Anderson put on the thirty-threes, and the recital started. It was going to be a while because I was the last dance number in act 2. The girls, helped by their moms, used the bathroom on the other side of the lobby to change into their many different costumes. I was feeling a bit giggly and happier since I'd taken those sips from the bottle. I didn't know a lot of the girls; I watched their moms rat and tease their hair and put lipstick on them. May was all fussed over. I think it was because she was overweight, and her family was trying to make her feel good.

I didn't change into my costume until act 2 started. When I heard the music for January, I decided to get into my tutu. By the time I came out of the bathroom, March was on. Four-eyed February got a lot of applause. I wondered if she'd danced without her glasses. I was proud to be December, the closing dance of the recital. Standing in the lobby, however, I felt totally un-Christmassy. Two weeks before Santa would come down the chimney, and

I was standing on a cold linoleum floor in a stiff yellow dress. Then I noticed the Christmas tree at the end of the lobby again. I hadn't really seen it before, with all the dancers dressing and scurrying about. Almost everyone was inside watching the second act. There were only about six of us in the hallway, and the tree was in full view.

It was a beautiful Christmas tree, with different colored bulbs, unbroken candy canes, silver tinsel, and hundreds of garlands of gold and shiny red ... Oops, I heard the music change again. Then there was a scratching sound, and the music started over. Miss Anderson had April doing acrobatics all over the stage. I had watched her practice. She was a tumbler, and her costume was pea green.

I waltzed over to the Christmas tree in time to the music, stretched out, and felt it. I even leaned in to smell the fresh pine, but it wasn't very fresh. Suddenly I got an idea. I looked at the tree and looked down at my three-quarter-length tutu, my bare legs, used ballet slippers, and my non-trimmed bodice. I felt like the little match girl standing outside the gift shop with all the storefront windows open. The angel hadn't appeared yet, so I knew I had time.

Swaying from side to side, I decided I'd make myself feel like Christmas. Uh oh! July was doing Yankee Doodle Dandy, so I had to hurry up with my shopping. Hmm, bulbs, yes, bulbs, I needed bulbs, and oh look, planes, tanks, and army men with shooters. I hooked medium-sized bulbs onto my skirt. Then I went around the back of the tree (I had about twenty-eight bulbs and characters on my skirt by then). I pulled gently on a red garland from back to front and entwined myself in it (it was three times as long as I was). I got a smaller silver one and wrapped it through my shoelace shoulder straps and around my neck. I tied it in a bow around my throat and let it hang down my back, like reins on a horse sleigh.

My tutu was red and green, the colors of the bulbs and tanks and bright balls. You could hardly see the squash color anymore. It felt great. I decided I had to have candy canes. I hooked them on top of my waistband and all over the top of my bodice. I didn't care that it was a little bit itchy. I draped silver tinsel all over the bulbs and ornaments. I stopped then, because my skirt was getting really heavy. I was beautiful. Now I *was* Christmas! Now I was truly who I was supposed to be. I was December in all its glory. Hallelujah! I didn't need any of that rich girls, cheap, sequined feather stuff.

By that point, October was midway through her routine, so I smiled and stood by the entrance door. I pointed my foot and did a couple of flexes and a few pliés. *I'm all warmed up*, I thought. Then I did a couple of slow pique turns so I wouldn't drop any tinsel. Everything stayed on except for a couple of strands. I knew I'd be okay. I felt magnificent. When it was close to the end of November's theme song, I prepared myself emotionally for my big entrance. I could see Loretta Anderson across the room exchanging November's record for mine. It was the "1812 Overture." She looked over at me, nodded, and put my music on.

She looked so elegant standing there in her high-heeled, black, sling-back pumps, coral-painted nails and lipstick, bleached white pony tail, and Barbie-like hair. She was going to love me. I was going to show them all. I didn't need to be rich to be Christmas.

My music started and the tinny record machine blared. I waited two counts before I pointed and piqued to the pulsing rhythm of the Pittsburg Philharmonic. Up and down I went, up and down, and the faster I piqued, the louder the music got. There were pops and crashes, more than I remembered but I thought it was just my excitement mixed with the finale's music. I finished my half-moon and went back toward the center of the dance floor for my final pirouette. The music skipped, and the needle slid and scratched off the record. Then I heard Loretta Anderson swearing.

Stopping mid-spin, I focused on the floor, because I was a bit woozy from Mama's water and my twirling turns. I had lost my spot, as they say in the dance world. As my eyes focused, I looked down at my tutu skirt and it wasn't the same costume I had when I came in. It looked like an old, dried-out Christmas tree, with empty prongs and broken candy canes hanging off my bodice and all over the floor. Silver tinsel littered the entire first row and the silver garland that had trailed so neatly down my neck was lying on the floor next to my right slipper. I looked over at Miss Anderson and saw that the long red garland had entwined itself around one of her pumps. Lifting my head to look into the audience, I saw no one there, only the remnants of broken Christmas balls. For an instant I thought the audience had vanished. I really wished that the angel would come for me then, because I certainly wasn't selling any matches. Then I saw frightened eyes peering over the tops of the metal chairs.

Slowly, people started to sit back up, cough, and adjust in their seats. Miss Anderson clip-clopped over to where I was swaying, pinched me by the ear, and dragged me toward the hallway door. Then I heard someone was clapping way back in the room, almost in the dark, clapping big, solid, full-hand claps. Before I reached the door, I turned to look, and my eyes filled with tears. Just moments before I had been filled with the spirit of Christmas, was inspired and in awe; and then I was humiliated and embarrassed. I squinted to see who was clapping. It wasn't Mama, who was helping to pick up the broken candy canes, and I didn't know anyone else. Then I saw him. It was my daddy. He was standing alone, clapping and smiling. His outline came into form as he stepped into the now-lit recreation room. In one of his big hands, he held the biggest candy cane I ever saw, with a huge red ribbon tied to it. When I saw his face and his arms outstretched, I knew it had all been worth it.

25

The Red Sweater

Winter 1964

"Mama! Stop!" I yelled out from the back seat as our brand-new, two-toned powder blue and white Chevy fish-tailed around the corner.

It was way past our bedtime, and Mama, Johnny, Darren, and I were on our way back to our newly painted and much larger Magnolia farmhouse. We had been to a pool party and spaghetti dinner at the Martins' house. They were friends of our new stepfather, Phil Taylor. I was in sixth grade.

They had one son older than Johnny and I and lived on a hill in a place called Sand Point. Mr. and Mrs. Martin's house was fancy. They even had a sign in the small bathroom off the swimming pool that read: *We Don't Swim in Your Toilet—So Don't PEE in Our POOL!*

It seemed a long way from where we lived, especially on that night. Even the windshield wipers had a hard time with the rain.

Our new stepfather, who had only been a member of

our family for three weeks, couldn't make the Martins' party. Mama told us after supper that he had a special story to put down before the newspaper could start rolling. He was a newspaper man and worked where the top of the world sat on the brown building in downtown Seattle. I could see it really bothered Mama because she kept going over to the silver ice bucket and laughed and giggled loudly as she filled her tall glass with ice again and again.

Mama really slurred her words in the car. It was hard to understand her. She just kept looking back at me trying to talk. It felt like she was paying more attention to Darren and me than on watching the car's lights were pointing.

"Now, Robin," Mama coaxed, like a front tooth waiting for the string pull. "Dahling, it would please your new daddy if, when you go back to school in September, you used his last name. He's adopting you and Darren because you're a girl and Darren is so young. Johnny doesn't want to take the Taylor name and that's just fine with Phil. But you'll be married someday and have a different name so it doesn't matter anyhow."

I waved at Mama to turn around because other car lights were getting way too close to us. We were bumping up against the Green Lake curves and drain gutters. Then Mama hit something hard, and I saw Johnny's blonde flat-top jerk up sharp, and then the force slammed his shoulder into the side door.

"Ow, ouch," Johnny whined as Mama tried to get control of the spinning car.

Darren was unusually quiet and hung onto the bottom of my red sweater. It was my old favorite fuzzy with the seven daisy buttons. We were sliding all over the stiff leather seat when I saw it. Straight between our two headlights was the tallest, brownest telephone pole I had ever seen.

Mama's face suddenly froze in anticipation. No sound came from her lips or anywhere else. There were only quick images, flashcards of my life, flipping by in front of my eyes. The Rolodex of my life was punctuated by a thunderous sound; wood splinters and glass shards instantly filled the air.

I reached out and grabbed Darren's pant legs, wondering why he was flying out in front of me. Then something stopped him, and we both were jerked back into the seat. I felt his weight against my chest, but all the lights had gone out.

Time and the feeling of life went away. Then I woke up to the shrill sound of a horn. As I regained some sensation, I realized the awful blare was coming from inside our car.

There were lights and men in big funny hats. People with umbrellas tried to peer in. Policemen yelled orders and passed a blanket through Mama's open window.

Darren was looking up at me when I opened my eyes. His nose was bleeding, so I pulled off my sweater and tried to wipe his face and lips clean. But the blood wouldn't stop. I was glad my sweater was red because then he wouldn't see the blood and get scared. Darren was a good little brother. He was calm. So was I. I just kept telling him that he was okay and that he had a silly old bloody nose, just like the kind Johnny always got.

Mama was crushed up tight against the steering wheel.

She was moaning and trying to turn her head toward a man in a dark-blue slicker. I couldn't make out what she was saying because the horn was still stuck.

Where was Johnny? I couldn't see him. Then a fireman outside my wrinkled door said something about a child trapped between the dashboard and the front seat. I was with Darren and could see Mama. *It must be Johnny*, I thought.

The thick telephone pole had pulled the car's front grill back to the middle just like center of a paper heart. My left leg was pinned between it and the backseat. Sparks flew as a rain-drenched man tried to saw open my door. There were soft, thudding sounds as he punched out the remaining window glass. Big gloved hands reached in, and someone asked me to hand him my little brother.

I didn't know or trust him. I said his name was Darren Schillereff, that I was his big sister, and we lived in a new house in Magnolia.

A kind face appeared at my window. He told me I was a very good big sister and that I'd surely want the best for Darren. He said there were wonderful nurses and doctors over by the flashing lights, who would take care of him, and that I could join him as soon as they cut me out of the car.

I carefully wrapped Darren in my sweater and passed him to the big fireman, who carefully lifted him out through the window, and then he was gone.

As I turned back toward the front seat, the car horn whimpered and then died out. People were working on all our doors, and a policeman was trying to ask Mama questions. She told him she didn't know what happened, but she still sounded sloshed to me. Couldn't he tell? Couldn't he smell how drunk she was?

Through the glare of the working lights I saw our stepfather, Phil, trying to get near the door where Mama was. His face was white, and he was trying to talk to the policeman. Everything started to close in on me, the noise, the splattering rain coming in from the back window. I shut my eyes and didn't come to till I woke up in the hospital emergency room.

We all survived. Darren had a concussion and thirty-two stitches across his forehead. Mama had some broken ribs, cuts, and a bruised face. Johnny was in the hospital the longest, with a broken arm and some internal bleeding. I escaped with a mild fracture and a leg full of oily, telephone-pole splinters.

They never fined Mama for driving drunk.

26

The Yellow Bikini

Summer 1966

For the second year in a row, our family had gotten to use a free Cadillac convertible. Each side advertised the Pat Boone Celebrity Golf Classic at Ocean Shores. It was a beautiful yellow car, and we kept the top down. One day Mama, Johnny, Darren, and I were going to Lake Washington to go swimming. My boyfriend at the time, Teddy, a very popular ninth-grader, was coming along with us. I had been going steady with him for two months. He gave me a Saint Christopher medal on a silver chain and called me at least once a week. In junior high, that meant we were a hot item. We would meet at parties and always did the slow dances together. We were definitely going steady.

On this particular Saturday, I had on my first grown-up bikini. It was bright shiny yellow. It wasn't a string bikini. It wasn't a tiny bikini, but it was my first two-piece and I felt very naked in it. It showed off my developing breasts and belly button. Wearing it gave me an exciting and awkward feeling.

Teddy had come over before lunch, and we were out on the porch talking. Then Mama came out and said, "Now Ted, y'all better go on up and tinkle 'cause you never know when you'll have to go again." I was mortified. I couldn't believe she had said that to a ninth-grader, especially this ninth-grader. Ted was vice president of his class. Thank goodness, he took it in a good way. He shrugged and went on upstairs. We quietly laughed, nudged elbows, and giggled about it later in the car.

It was about noon when we drove north over the Ballard Bridge on our way toward Lake Washington. Mom had been driving all morning, so our drive was a little uncertain. In and out, she'd weave through the traffic, her head a little wobbly. But with Johnny in the front seat, ready to grab the wheel, if necessary, and Teddy and Darren in the back with me, I felt safe. We were all ready for the beach. We had our towels, our balls, our sunscreen, and even a packed lunch.

When we finally arrived in the crowded parking lot, everyone pointed at our car, thinking that Pat Boone had arrived. When they took a good look, they saw that he wasn't there. It was a gorgeous summer beach day, one of those perfect Seattle blue days. After unpacking the car in a spot that Mom had picked out, Teddy and I ran for the shore. I ran ahead so he wouldn't see my boobies bounce. I still felt kind of shy. We swam and swam to a raft about a hundred yards off the sandy shore. Teddy and I teased, splashed, and played all the way out to it. He was a lot of fun. There were two diving boards on the floating raft.

One was regular pool size and the other stuck out from a soft ladder. Teddy and I dove off both of them. Lake Washington was really muddy so if we jumped off the twelve-foot diving board, our feet kind of got stuck in the bottom for just a split second, but we could always manage to kick up through.

It was a perfect day for young love. We must have been swimming and roasting at least three hours when Teddy and I felt really hungry. It was the kind of swimming hunger where we had to eat then or we thought we'd faint or die. So we swam to shore. We grabbed Darren, who was playing with his shovel and pail, and brought him with us. We couldn't see Johnny. I was sure he was still swimming or getting into some trouble. We walked through the shore crowd, past the sunbathers, and on up through the picnic tables. We headed just north of where the car was parked in the lot near the little grassy knoll to where we had left Mama.

As we walked toward her, we saw a huge crowd. I asked Teddy if he could see anything. He was tall and big as a bear. He couldn't, so he stepped out in front of me and, like a bulldozer, plowed right through the circle of people. It was the first time I ever saw hair on the back of a man. Well, he wasn't really a man, he was only in the ninth grade; yet, the boy was a man. I was caught off-guard, and I let out a blood-curdling scream. The crowd jumped and then divided. People stared at Teddy and me. He was red from head to toe, and I was pale white in my yellow bikini. Teddy was so sweet, he just let the embarrassment roll off him, and then he took my hand and turned back toward Mama.

As we stepped through the opening in the crowd, I saw that about seven little boys and I think even a little girl were tossing pebbles into my mother's open mouth. I guess she'd been snoring, completely stoned out of her mind, sprawled out on the blanket. I had no idea how long this had been going on. Teddy quickly shooed and kicked the kids away and broke up the crowd. I started to cry. I was so ashamed. Seeing my mother incoherently snoring, while strange kids tossed pebbles in her mouth was a nightmare. Thank goodness Teddy was there. He was my knight in shining armor. He had his driver's permit and proudly drove my family home, drooling mother and all. It was the first and last time I wore that yellow bikini.

27

Blue Suede Clogs

Late Summer 1968

It was a beautiful early August morning. I took the bus downtown from Magnolia to go to the Piccoli Stage Cartoon Company, where I worked as an usher, props hand, and sometime cartoon character. I walked through the Seattle Center, near the Seattle Pacific Science Center building. The soft summer breeze blended with the scent of lilac blooms and the spray from the fountains. Walking around the display of international flags, I turned south to the Food Circus. It was a big square building with international stores in the basement and a funny glass, space-age elevator that went up to the second floor.

The weekend before, a desperate woman had jumped off the Space Needle. She died on the cement below, near the monorail entrance. I didn't want to go around that part, even though it was a shorter walk to the theater. I could still see those men in the green shirts with the Space

Needle sewn on the pockets hosing down the cement where she fell.

That summer my mother had enrolled me in the Piccoli Stage Cartoon Company summer theater program. She was hoping it would help my shyness and stuttering. For a few years, I'd been having trouble saying anything that started with "d" or "t," especially at home. I usually just answered, "Yes, ma'am. No ma'am. No sir. Yes sir." I tried to do what I was told to do, and if I could sneak away, I would. But I was really thankful that Mom had enrolled me in this theater program. It got me out of the house and was a real creative outlet for me.

I helped seat the small children during the kiddy shows and swept up the peanuts after the evening adult melodramas. I was mesmerized by the whole process—the audience, the cast, and the way it was all set up. After I graduated from the eight-week children's theater program, the company accepted me as an apprentice. Soon I had a role. I was Gwendolyn Goldfish in the new children's show. I was going to be a star. I was an actress and in love with everyone there. This was my new family, and I couldn't wait to get there every weekend. School was the only thing that stopped me from going everyday.

The Sea-fair Parade was the biggest Seattle summer event, except for the speedboat races on Lake Washington. I was going to march in the parade as Herby Mole, which had a furry brown costume with a mole's face and a hat with a big whirligig on top. I was supposed to wave at all the people and pass out balloons to the kids along the two-mile route. I got a whole lot of experience. I was also in the musical *The Unsinkable Molly Brown*, and I had eight different parts. It seemed all I did was change my costume, cross the stage, and then change again. It was fun. I was sixteen and couldn't help but be busy all the time. In addition, I earned getting five dollars a show at the Piccoli Stage Cartoon Company. I was secretly saving my money, so that when I was eighteen, I could move out of the house and rent my own apartment.

I was filled with anticipation and daydreaming as I walked through the bushy lane heading over to the theater. As I clumped along in my new clogs, I realized how sore the tops of my feet were. The previous week, with some money I had saved from my second paycheck and a little extra from my dresser drawer, I went down to the basement of the Food Circus to the Holland Shop, where I bought my first pair of clogs.

They were navy, square-toed clogs with white piping on the top edges. I'd had my eyes on them for at least two long months, ever since I'd graduated from the eight-week theater program. This was the second time I ever wore them, and it felt like I was wearing new ballerina pointe shoes. With the clogs, I had to go through the blister stage, just as I had in ballet class. Even thick socks didn't stop the hurt on top of the skin, but I was determined to be a clog wearer.

I was walking a little slower than usual and looked down at where I stepped. By the time I did look up, I realized how quiet it had gotten. There were no people that I could see, and even the sound of the cars had faded out. It was like someone had pulled a plug, and it all drained away. Everything got sucked into the silence. A weird feeling went up my spine. It reminded me of when

the birds stopped chattering before the earthquake we'd
had a few years back.

Suddenly out of nowhere, an ugly man with a pock–
marked face barreled into me and shoved me straight into
the bushes. He fell on top of me; his stomach covered
my entire body. His breath was loud, raspy, and he spit
as he breathed. I wasn't frightened; I just went to a cool
unemotional place. All I could think about was not losing
my new clogs, even though I felt him ripping and tearing
at my blouse. I didn't feel my body, and I didn't feel any
pain, I just felt his weight rolling from side to side on top
of me.

One of my clogs was pressed under my butt. My
left foot was bare. I didn't care that he had ripped open
my blouse and was pulling up my slip, but I was furious
that I might lose my new shoes. The branches broke and
snapped all around me as he rolled over me and tried
to put me on my stomach. Quickly, I reached for my
clog, and I started to beat on his back and his head. My
fists were flying. There were no more sounds, just the
vibrations of hits on someone's body.

Then as quickly as they had faded out, voices started
to filter in. There were honks and beeps and loud car
whoosh noises. Where had they all been? It was like
someone had turned on the lights in a dark room. Then
as suddenly as he'd assaulted me, the ugly man with the
hot, spitting breath was gone.

Looking down into the dirt, I sat back up on my
haunches and realized what had happened. My clean
white blouse was torn open and my red–flowered skirt was
smudged with wet dirt and sticky leaves. I reached for the

clog that I had hit him with and saw, as I turned around, the other one still in the middle of the white brick lane. I didn't really think about what had happened, only that I was going to be late for the Sea-fair Parade.

Standing up in the bushes, I waited till some people walked on by. Brushing myself off, I tucked in what remained of my blouse into my skirt, and stepped out and picked up my other shoe. The first people I passed didn't even notice my lone clog. They were so into taking pictures of the Space Needle. I was glad and avoided the gaze of another older tourist couple walking toward me. I was numb. I don't remember feeling anything, not even the oozing open blisters under my socks. I just walked, ghostlike, in the direction of the Piccoli Stage Cartoon Company.

I must have had a different look about me, because when I finally got to the theater, someone asked, "Robin, are you all right? You look so pale." I told them I was fine. I don't remember saying much. I went to get into my furry mole costume and got ready for the parade.

At that time, I didn't absorb what had happened. I wrapped it up and put it away with all the other tightly sealed packages. I didn't think about it for years. That was the only time I ever bought a pair of clogs.

28

$1.06 Wedding

August 17, 1970

I left home May of my junior year in high school. Once Mom had enrolled me in that theater program at the Piccoli Stage Cartoon Company, I became involved in a lot of other community theater projects. I worked for the Lyric Theater, Seattle Junior Programs, and in high-school plays. I'd been saving my spare money so I could get my own place.

My first apartment was near Queen Anne High, about eight blocks from where I was going to school. It was in the basement of an old Victorian red-shingled house. The owner was very nice to me. She told me her daughter had lived in the apartment when she went to the University of Washington. She was gone, so the woman was on her own. She rented it out so she could make a little money and not be so lonely.

My apartment was really cute. The kitchen had a little electric hot plate and a baby refrigerator. There was a kind of living room with a coffee table and green plaid couch.

The bedroom was so tiny, there was only a foot between the bed and the wall. The chest of drawers only had two openings, the top two drawers. It was a pretty tight room, but it was mine so I didn't care. The bathroom was at the other end of the basement, opposite the washer and dryer. But for sixty-five dollars a month, it was worth it.

During my junior year, I met my first husband, Eric. He was a senior at the time. He had qualities that reminded me, in good ways, of my father. He was tall and lanky, sort of like Gary Cooper in *Pride of the Yankees*. Evidently, he had fallen for me pretty hard. I liked him, but I really didn't know how I felt about him.

School was hard work, and work was hard, and I didn't seem to be really getting anywhere. I didn't even have enough food to eat. I read in the paper that, if you were married, for fifty cents you could get fifty-two dollars in food stamps. With Boeing and Lockheed on strike and the bread lines pretty long (even at the Sunbeam Bakery down at the bottom of the hill), that sounded pretty good to me.

It was late August, right before my senior year. Eric's family lived off Fifteenth Street near the motorcycle shop under the Magnolia Bridge. Ever since the spring production of *Li'l Abner,* Eric had been asking me to marry him. His parents had married young and had nine kids, so he was used to living on a lower-level income. I liked him. He was kind, handsome, and knew how to drive a motorcycle. So one day I finally said, "Okay, let's get married."

That August we were performing in *Are There Alligators in the Sewers of the City of New York*. It was the children's show before Richard Chamberlain's matinee performance of *Richard II* at Seattle Rep. Eric and I were also involved in a musical project called *Cash*, which employed Seattle kids to get them off the streets. Between performances at the children's show, the Piccoli Stage Cartoon Company, and the Junior Programs, I got married.

I borrowed twenty-five dollars to get married from an older man with whom I had worked in a community theater show. Then Eric and I looked for a justice of the peace in the Yellow Pages. There must have been more than eight pages of them, so I picked one at random. I flipped through, pointed my finger down, opened my eyes, and read the name. I was astonished to find out years later that I picked the very same justice of the peace who had married my mother and stepfather. It's funny how things work out.

We called and made an appointment. The magistrate said we had to get a license and blood test, so we went downtown and took care of that. We went to the Queen Anne pharmacy the Saturday before and looked at all the rings on that finger pole. I bought a wedding band that cost $1.06 with tax. It was silver and looked real pretty on my finger. Eric didn't want one.

The big day came a week later. It was a Monday, and I had a white dress that I had borrowed—well, stolen—from my mother's closet. It was a dress that a rich Magnolia lady who had a swimming pool had given her. I knew it didn't fit her, so I didn't feel so bad. Eric wore blue jeans and a white short-sleeved turtleneck. It was August 17, 1970. We went over to the Interbay side of Magnolia, where the justice of the peace lived. We got there at 10 a.m., thinking that was our appointment time. When he answered the door, the justice of the peace was in his bathrobe, as was his wife. I must have heard the wrong time on the phone. He'd said 2 p.m. They were in the process of moving, so the room was littered and stacked with boxes.

The only people who knew about this marriage were Eric's brothers and family. We waited while the justice of the peace and his wife got dressed. The only friend of mine who came was the man from whom I had borrowed the twenty-five dollars. Later, Eric's oldest brother, Ken, paid him back. He was always kind and generous that way. Ken even went to White Front and got me a real wedding band, a silver ring that cost a whole thirty dollars. It was something.

We got married that day. I kissed all his brothers and my friend and then Eric, and we went to the Seattle Center. We spent the whole day going on rides and holding hands. We kissed by the half-moon spiked fountain near the coliseum. It was the first and only time I heard explosions in my head. I thought fireworks were going off, but when I opened my eyes, it was a clear night. Everyone should have a kiss like that in their lifetime. All in all, it was a great wedding day.

Then I went back to my little sixty-five dollar a month apartment, and Eric went back to his house. We didn't room together or live together until it was almost Christmas that senior year. By December everybody knew I was married. All my friend's mothers were waiting for my stomach to grow. A few of my good friends stuck by me, but the rest were told not to see me anymore. I guess it was odd. I never dated and then all the sudden, I was married.

We went to the senior prom as "Mr. and Mrs." When the man introduced us, he whispered, "Congratulations." I giggled. We'd already been married nearly a whole year. But the exciting thing was, when I graduated, my entire class and their parents gave me a standing ovation.

As it turned out, you could get a high-school diploma, get married, and not be pregnant. Yep, my stomach never grew. Eric and I stayed together for fourteen years. It all started because of food stamps, friendship, and a plain, old $1.06 wedding ring.

29

Plasma Day at the Woolworth's Counter

Winter 1971

It was one week before Christmas 1970. Eric and I had been married since August, but this was the first time we were actually living together. It was a three-story wooden house between Magnolia and Queen Anne Hill, an old turn-of-the-century Victorian just off Fifteenth Street. Five us shared this weathered, old house, three of whom were Eric's brothers. The rent was *very* reasonable. We each paid $12.50 a month. The house was kind of rundown, but we didn't care.

Eric and I had spent the last week repainting one of the third-floor rooms. It had a fireplace and it was the perfect bedroom for a newly married couple. Unfortunately, one of Eric's older brothers, during his acid trip days in the late 1960s, had painted the room in neon-colored sperm tails. It took two gallons of white oil-based paint to even begin to kill them. From our repainted iron wrought bed, it still looked like some of them were still moving under the paint. All in all, Eric and I worked very hard to make the room fit for *House and Garden.*

On our first night together, we spent the last of the change from Eric's unemployment check on two Presto Logs. They were the rage at the time. It had been a really rough December and had been snowing nonstop for two days. We thought it looked pretty outside our plastic-covered windows. Eric and I lit the logs and pulled up the six ratty blankets for our first wedded night's bliss. Suddenly, even before the paper around the Presto Log burned, the ice-laden roof caved in. Rotted shingles, snow mounds, and flying plastic fell all over the room. We jumped up, grabbed the blankets and our boxes of clothes, and dragged them out the door. We ended up storing our clothes near the second-floor dining room. Because there was no central heat, all of us slept in the kitchen. That winter we kept three thick army blankets over the kitchen door. We all got used to it, and it was a comfortable place. We lit the gas oven for heat.

It was a rough time in Seattle. With the Vietnam War raging, tempers and unemployment seemed to be at an all time high. Every church collected food products. It wasn't only the needy and missions that needed the help, normal families did too. It was a really bad Christmas for many.

I was a senior in high school, and Eric had been laid off as an usher the previous month because attendance at movie theaters was so low, especially in downtown Seattle. People weren't shopping or going out on dates. We hadn't eaten in about three days. Eric's brothers rode motorcycles over to eastern Washington to visit their folks, who had moved out of Seattle. It was a scary time, and we all were very possessive about our food. His brothers' food cabinets were locked while ours hung open and were completely empty.

Eric and I decided to go down to the blood bank near Pioneer Square. I had read in the *Queen Anne Weekly* that they were looking for plasma donors. They would take two pints, and we'd get double the money. It sounded easy, so we said "Great, let's do it." We had to walk downtown because we didn't even have trolley or bus money. It was a really icy-cold day.

The blood bank was on the southwest corner of Pioneer Square in the old area known as Skid Row, where they used to roll the logs down into the Sound. It was pretty empty and desolate that morning. A few hobos and bums smoked and drank near the blood bank door. *This is going to be an interesting event*, I thought. Eric and I walked into the blood-donation center. Men in tattered clothes, drunk or acting sober, stood in a line in front of us. We waited. There were all kinds of people: Eskimos, mothers with nursing babies, army guys, and a lot of homeless men. There were kids our age too. But most looked older than we were, and many were in different stages of sobriety. It was a pretty rough part of town.

Eric and I had our middle fingers pricked and tested. "Have you had any alcoholic beverage in the past twenty-four hours?" a short nurse asked tiredly without looking up. Both of us replied "no" at the same time. We were then weighed and our blood-pressure levels checked. I liked the squish- squish feeling of the pump around my upper arm. It made me feel like a weight lifter. We then were led to "lie down" tables in a big room. There were at least eight bodies between us. Some were snoring and a scruffy man on my right had sour breath that reminded me of my mother in church, so I turned my head to face the other way.

The room had a wagon train feel, with beds in a circle, and nurses and needles on trays in the center. Underneath each bed was a machine that went clickity-clack, clickity-clack. The nurse explained that the machine prevented the blood from getting clotty and made it easier to take out the white blood cells. I felt okay. I didn't mind giving two pints of blood. I looked over the "sour breath man" and waved at Eric with my free arm. He squinted and smiled and gave me the OK sign. I knew he was a bit squeamish about needles, but he was doing just fine.

The blood-sucking process took an hour and a half, after which we got free orange juice and all the graham crackers we could eat. Then we signed a paper and each got seven dollars.

Crossing through Pioneer Square, Eric and I couldn't decide where to eat. So we walked up the hill toward the downtown area. A lot of restaurants looked inviting, but we knew they were much too expensive. We even looked in at Pike Street Market, but we were too tired to fix anything. Finally, we decided on the Woolworth's counter near the Bartell Drugstore under the monorail. It was cheap, and we'd get a lot of food. We were going to have a great meal. It would be just like a Christmas dinner. I remember they had a nice big menu. I was euphoric. We had fourteen dollars between us, and we were rich.

We walked through the glass double doors, past Woolworth's Christmas cookie tins section; hard-rock candy bags were everywhere. We went between the socks and vinyl handbags, turned left, and were at the middle of the lunch counter. It was pretty crowded because it was almost noon, and a lot of the people from nearby office buildings were grabbing a bite. We took two empty stools close to the front doors. I already knew what I wanted. Eric grabbed the laminated menu to pick his choice. I told a platinum-blonde, penciled-eyebrows waitress with Christmas tree earrings, "I'll have a toasted turkey club sandwich, please." Eric ordered the turkey dinner with raisin-nut dressing and a cranberry cup. We both ordered chocolate milk shakes.

Sitting on our backless swivel stools, we waited for our lunch. Christmas carols came out of the speakers on the ceiling above us. As we waited, I rocked to the familiar jingle melodies. All of a sudden, I felt a little light-headed. Maybe it was the holiday excitement. I said "Eric, I'm gonna go out and get some fresh air," and got up and walked over to the glass doors.

I stepped out onto the sidewalk. Bundled bodies with brightly wrapped packages criss-crossed around me. It smelled like snow was in the air. A diesel bus drove by and spewed fumes and smoke all over me. I still felt a little dizzy so I decided to go back in and sit down, thinking that the food should have been there by now.

I walked back to my empty seat. Eric was just starting to dig for his dressing underneath the sliced turkey and gravy as I sat down. I looked at my toasted club sandwich with the butter pickles on the side, felt a rush of nausea, and knew I was going to throw up. I was starting to get an attack of the black and whites. Even the lettuce on my club sandwich looked gray. I felt like all the blood from my head was sloshing around in my stomach. I knew I was going to faint, but I wanted Eric to eat his Christmas dinner, so I turned to him and said, "I'll be right back."

I stood up and looked for a place where I could faint. The only place that looked good was the four-for-a dollar photo booth. Just as I was going to part the curtain, I saw two pairs of shoes inside. *Well, not here*, I thought. By then I had broken out in a cold sweat, but the only place I could lie down was a small area on the other side of the booth. Unfortunately, if I passed out there, I might roll down the stairs into the basement.

Completely drenched in perspiration, I weaved back toward Eric. I crossed back very slowly; everything looked like a slow-moving X-ray. I slid onto my stool and took another look at my club sandwich. I stood up, turned violently, and that's the last thing I remember until I woke up in an elderly woman's comforting arms.

The two of us were sitting entwined in two folding chairs near the front door. A mustached store manager paced, very nervously, back and forth in front of us. He kept glancing over at me like he was waiting for something. Eric came up behind me with my coat and gloves, dropped them, and went outside. The kind old woman continued to stroke my hair as she gently rocking me back and forth. Soft color and light came into my eyes as she spoke. "You're going to be just fine," she said softly. "The first time is the hardest, and the first month the worst." I had no idea what she was talking about, but

151

her soothing words made me feel a lot better. It was only later on in the cab on the way home that I realized she must have thought I was pregnant.

Eric bounded back in and looked at me. He said to the store manager, "Thank you, thank you both, but we won't need an ambulance. We'll just take a cab home." The kind old woman and the store manager nodded and walked toward the back office. Thanking the sweet woman again, Eric and I left Woolworth's to wait on the snow-dusted sidewalk.

It didn't take long for the cab to arrive. All the way home, Eric described the fainting episode. He had just found his raisin-nut dressing with his fork when he heard a loud crack behind him. There I was, laid out flat, face down, stiff as a board. It sounded like I had split my head open or broken my nose, but when he and a man who was sitting next to me lifted me up, nothing was bleeding. People jumped up from their seats, as if they thought their food was poisoned or there was a strange plague creeping over the counter. Eric told me that people exited every which way. Some even stepped over me to get to the door. He said he was not only frightened but really angry. A store manager came out to help drag me to the now-propped-open front door for some fresh air. I was out cold.

Then this elderly woman from the far end of the lunch counter went over to the store manager and told him to go get two chairs, which he did. The store manager was so worried, he called an ambulance. About five minutes later, I woke up.

We spent the rest of our "blood money" on a cab

home. I never got one bite of that toasted turkey club, and Eric never tasted his raisin-nut dressing. I cannot write enough words to explain how much we laughed. Thank goodness that the Presbyterian Church in Magnolia had a pretty good canned food supply. We went over there, and the church people were so kind, they packed a whole box of food for us. It was more than enough to last us a whole week. We had Kraft Macaroni & Cheese, Libby's Pumpkin, Wonder Bread, three cans of cranberries, and lots of other stuff. It was more than fourteen dollars worth.

30

Soot and the Liquor-Store Boy

Winter 1973

Eric and I had been in college for two years in San Diego. It was Christmas 1973, and we were finally going home. We had a 1957 VW bug; "Mormon," we called her, because we had purchased her from an elderly Mormon woman back in Seattle. I was a little nervous about going to Mama and Phil's new house. The weather was pretty rough all the way north on I-5.

When Darren left to go into the Air Force, and with Johnny still in Vietnam, there was no reason to hold onto the farmhouse on Thirty-third Street. So Mama and Phil bought a smaller house overlooking Interbay, and they invited us home for the holidays.

We had to save some of our work-study money, so we had just enough to drive up for a visit and go over the Cascades to Cashmere to see his folks too. We got to Seattle pretty late. It must have been after 9 p.m. the day before Christmas Eve.

The rain was really pouring. It was hard to see through Mormon's worn-out wipers, but I finally found the house. I kept telling Eric that my mother had a few peculiarities, but he always thought of her as nice. To him, she was so Southern and charming. I never told him about her drinking. I said she used to drink, but I never really said how much.

Without an umbrella, we climbed up the long cement stairs to the front door. It looked like a cute house, even though it was a lot smaller than the one on Thirty-third Street. I rang the bell. The door was cracked open a bit, and I could hear the vacuum cleaner going. I turned to Eric behind me and said, "Let's just go in. She's probably vacuuming and can't hear us." I opened the screen door and pushed open the front door. There in the little living room that I had never seen before was my mother. She was lying on her back, and the vacuum cleaner nozzle was blowing the fireplace soot all over the room.

Coughing through the soot, Eric and I stepped into the living room. He shut off the Electrolux, and I went over to face Mama. She was rolling in the soot, laughing hysterically and trying to get up. She turned over when she saw me, her face all covered in soot, and drawled, "Dahlin', what are you doing here? I wasn't expecting you till, oh my, what time is it?" She was trying to get up but kept slipping. I was so embarrassed. Maybe at least now Eric would understand what a bad drinker she was.

Trying to hold her up, I got soot and dirt all over me. I put her down on her dirty Queen Ann chair and went to find a towel. All the while she kept repeating, "Dahlin', what are you doin' here?" I soaked a hand towel from the bathroom, went back in, and started to wipe off her face and hands. From behind me, I heard the vacuum cleaner go back on. Eric was trying to clean up some of the mess in the room.

After I wiped Mama off, I started to wash myself. I went into the kitchen and turned on the full kettle to make some instant coffee. As I was searching the cupboards for cups, I heard the doorbell chime: "Ding-dong, ding-dong," Mama said as she tried to stand up. "Oh, dahlin', I'll get it. It's just a package I'm waiting for."

I said, "No, Mom, I'll get it."

I went out of the small kitchen and stepped into the cleaned living room, but Eric had already opened the door. Standing between the screen in the dripping doorway was a young boy wearing a Christmas scarf and a baseball hat. He was holding a cardboard box. I knew by the bottle-cap reflection caused by the porch light that he was the liquor-store boy. I couldn't believe it. "Shit!"

I felt Mom pushing behind me. She said, "Let me take care of it, darlin'." She searched for her purse around the sofa.

Eric and I didn't have enough money to pay for all the bottles of vodka, so we let Mama pay. Eric was nice enough to give the liquor-store boy a nice tip, though. I always did like that about him. He closed the door with his foot and walked the box full of bottles into the kitchen and slid it across the table. He gave a knowing look and nodded at Mom. We both watched her sashay into the kitchen, weaving and heading toward the bottles. Eric left me with her and continued to clean the living room.

Hot angry tears welled up into my eyes. I looked at Mama and said in a choking voice, "How could you? How could you? We haven't been home in two years and this is what we come home to?"

"Oh darlin', it's just for the holidays," she slurred. "You know how it is, Robin Rae. We're gonna have some people over."

I cut her off. "I'm gonna make you something to eat." Taking her by the shoulders, I maneuvered her out the kitchen door. "Go," I said, "and put some clean clothes on. You're a mess."

Mumbling and walking away, she said, "Oh darlin', you're just too early. I wasn't expecting you until Christmas."

Alone in the kitchen, one by one I started opening the bottles and emptying them. There were seven in all, each one a big half-liter. Sobs engulfed me, and memories flooded back. I thought this was over. Eric must've heard me because he turned off the vacuum cleaner and came into the kitchen. He knew how angry I was because this was a different Robin, one he'd never seen.

I left only one full bottle and stacked the other empty six near the garbage. Mama returned, and she was furious. Her arms swung through the air, and she swore. I could see that she was trying to hold herself back, but she couldn't. Pushing Eric out of the kitchen, she said sweetly, "Now, darlin', why don't you go out into the living room and help finish the tree, and I'll make us something to eat." There was a dark and bitter edge to her voice. Exhausted, I left the full half-liter on the counter and followed Eric into the living room.

"Eric, I can't stay, I just can't." Tears rolled down my cheeks.

He sat next to me. "Robin, let's wait until your dad gets home tomorrow. Let's just wait. We're tired; we've been driving all day. Let's get something to eat. We can't just leave. Tomorrow's Christmas Eve."

I don't know how long Eric comforted me, but it was enough time for Mama to warm up some beans and franks or a Sloppy Joe mix, I'm not sure which. But I do remember Mama coming out of the kitchen holding a steaming bowl. She weaved toward Eric and stood on the mauve carpet about two feet from his wet shoes. The she said in that sweet, sticky drawl of hers, with her eyes batting toward him, "I know how all you farm boys like to eat. You're used to eatin' off the floor." And she put the bowl down.

I shot up. Trying not to cry, I grabbed Eric's hand, ripped my coat off the back of the chair, and stormed out the front door into the wet snow.

I drove nonstop all the way to Cashmere, over the Cascade Mountains and through the blinding snow. It took the rest of the night. I cried and shook the entire way. I heard nothing but my own raging thoughts. For the first time, Eric understood why I had kept so quiet about my family.

That was the only time I set foot in that little house. I didn't see my mother or stepfather again until the summer of 1974.

31

Broken Glasses

Spring 1974

It was late, almost 8:20 on a beautiful May night in San Diego. The smell of jasmine and honeysuckle blooms in nearby Balboa Park came in warm pockets through my open window. It was that time of day between fickle dusk and deep purple night.

Eric and I attended USIU, and it was only a block and a half away from our downtown apartment on Second Avenue and Cedar Street. The wooden, four-story apartment complex was one house from the corner and right across from the Cedar Street off-ramp and a lipstick-looking Holiday Inn.

I was in charge of props for our school's main stage production of *The Rainmaker*, and had to be there no later than 8:30 p.m. I had to arrive well before the start of act 2 so I could make sure the aluminum sheets for making the thunder noise were in place.

This was my second year of college. My hair was styled in a boy cut, à la Peter Pan. I wore thin, round, gold-wire glasses that could be bent back into shape if someone sat on them, which I somehow managed to do a lot. That's why I liked them. Eric and I didn't have a lot of money to spend on "necessities," so we were really practical.

Quickly, I threw on my *South Pacific* jumpsuit and laced up my old sneaks. I locked the single bolt behind me, bounded down the three flights of stairs, hopped the two front steps, and skipped across Second Avenue.

Walking along the Cedar Street sidewalk, I hurried toward the school. On my right was the half-block, stone-gravel parking lot used by the parishioners of Saint Joseph's. Against its high, pink-stucco wall, the vacant lot looked smaller in the evening shadows. I could just barely make out a few early stars above the eucalyptus trees in the park. A few songbirds sang on the wires above me.

"Excuse me," came a male voice from behind me. "Have you seen a little white dog?"

"What?" I replied, taken aback by how suddenly this tall dark man had appeared from out of nowhere. I was not sure I heard him right so I asked again. "I'm sorry, what did you say?" I was ill at ease.

The man was right next to me and looking all around at my feet. Out of the corner of my eye, I caught a glimpse of a rusted, maroon low-rider creeping along the curb. Somehow, the tall dark man had gotten behind me; he seemed to be trying to show me how tiny the dog was. Suddenly something took my breath away, and I felt very light. I realized that I had been grabbed and was being forced toward the car. I kicked frantically.

As I struggled to free myself, the man went for my

throat but caught my glasses instead. As he pressed down hard, the glasses bent at the nose and a lens popped out. *Not my glasses!* I screamed inside my head. Now I was mad. Slicing my right cheek, they fell to the ground.

The car door swung open, and I saw a glint of steel against the seat. Slipping from his hold on me, I fell forward. A big calloused hand covered my mouth as the other lifted me toward the door. There was movement in the backseat. That meant there were at least three of them. If the tall dark man got me in the car, I'd be dead. Fight! FIGHT!

My free leg swung and hit the roof of the car. I couldn't believe that this was happening. The man tried to push me into the car; like an accordion, I was in and out, in and out. I could smell his sour alcohol breath as he grunted and forced his weight on me. It was like a bad Keystone cops movie. I was laughing inside because I was trying to save myself with my weak left leg. It was especially lazy after our jazz class that day, which had been devoted entirely to Luigi's style and thigh hinges. But then I felt the knife.

My dangling right leg had been gashed by the man in the front seat. Kicking against empty air, I lifted my right knee up with all my might and slammed it against the edge of the roof. With both legs, I bent and pushed back as hard as I could.

We fell back over the sidewalk and onto the gravel. The tall dark man had one hand on my jumpsuit. As I scrambled to get up, some of my stainless steel buttons ripped off. My white undershirt was spotted with blood and rocks as I tried to roll over and get up. Climbing up on all fours, I took off. I was almost standing when my worn–out sneaker caught a stone and tripped me, and I fell face down. Spitting dirt and tasting blood, I could hear men's voices behind me, cursing and speaking English and Spanish, and they were getting closer. None of this made any sense, but I knew I had to run for my life.

I struggled to get up again, but a heavy weight stopped me. Trying to get away from the suffocating pressure, I rolled onto my back using my elbows. I started to scream, but a hand came from behind me and stuffed my mouth with something. I gagged and choked as I was dragged back on my butt closer and closer to the back wall of Saint Joseph's.

I heard something tear but didn't know what it was. Crawling like a crab and backwards, I tried to keep the sweating man in the hat from touching me. As I stumbled up again to a standing position, I saw that I was in the middle of the darkening parking lot. The maroon low-rider was now crunching slowly over the gravel and coming toward me. With the tall dark man pulling me back and the man in the hat covering me, there was no way I could be seen from the street. It was getting hard to breathe. The rag was sticking to my dry throat. Something white shone from the driver's seat as the car moved toward me. Where were all the people? Where were all the cars?

I didn't believe I was going to die as long as I didn't get in the car, but I had little chance of escape now. Hitting the church wall with my back, I glance down and saw that my entire chest was exposed. Funny, I had no sensation of good or bad. That must have been what that tearing sound was. I suddenly felt physically exhausted, but my mind was looking for escape.

The car stopped about six feet from my shoes. The driver's door opened slowly and a third man got out. With his body silhouetted against the street lights, I could see that he was from the military. He stood tall in his Navy dress whites. I'll always remember the three stripes on his sleeve and the scent of his sickly sweet cologne.

Without warning, a hand jerked at my clothes while another kicked me to the ground. The man in the dress whites just watched and stood silent. Then there was a gush of air between my thighs and someone's sticky skin on my back. The last thing I felt were rocks cutting through my palms, shin, and knees.

I floated up and free. I drifted high and looked around. I saw the roof of our apartment building and the Holiday Inn. I saw a small commotion in the parking lot next to the church. Cedar Street was spotted with a few cars.

I am not sure how long I lay there. I heard myself take a breath and knew I was alive. How alive, I wasn't sure. The sound of moving and crunching gravel roused me to open my swollen eyes. Then I saw the maroon low-rider scrape bottom and drive off the curb. Cars were everywhere now. Three in a row got off the exit ramp. "Run, Robin, run, now's your chance."

Forcing myself to stand, I wobbled and pulled up my limp and bloody jumpsuit. Using the wall for support, I pushed myself toward Second Avenue. I used my feet to feel for my glasses. The maroon car saw me at the corner and stopped. They tried to make a U-turn on the one way but a speeding car roared off the freeway ramp, just missed the low-rider, and screeched to a stop. The sound caught my attention. They're still here. "Run, run for your life, Robin."

The adrenaline kicked in, and I shot off. With four long strides I made the sidewalk, but in the dark and without my glasses I overran the curb and skidded chest-first into the street. It felt like I just erased my nipples. *Stupid, Robin, really stupid. Quick, get up. Get up before they turn the corner.*

Peeling myself off the concrete, I crossed the street and ran for the underpass, down the one-way, past the ramp. I turned left and back up the street behind our apartment building. I jumped over the rusted chain-link fence and through the overgrown backyard. A church bell rang:

ONE—Hurry, hurry before they see you.

TWO—Lift your legs faster, faster.

THREE—Another landing.

FOUR—Where's your key? It's gone.

FIVE—Try the door; stay low so they can't see you.

SIX—Hurry, try the window. Harder, harder.

SEVEN—It's opening, push.

EIGHT—Squeeze in now. Faster, faster.

NINE—Melt down onto the hardwood floor.

I peered out the window, but there was nothing, I saw nothing. No maroon car was waiting. I was safe. I had made it. Robin had made it. Crawling to our apartment door, I lay huddled like a fetus and waited for Eric to come home.

32

Mother, McDonalds, and the Old Globe

1974

In 1974, I got my first Equity contract at the Old Globe Theater. It was LORT D, an equity contract at $135.50 a week. I was a union actress! The theater was actually adjacent to the Globe; it was called the Cassius Carter. It was a wonderful experience. I had responsibilities and creative challenges. During that summer, Phil was down to cover a gold tournament at Torrey Pines. He was a marvelous sports writer. He wrote for a Seattle newspaper and occasionally for *Sports Illustrated.* My mother accompanied him on this trip; they were staying at the Hilton near Mission Bay.

Eric was a spear-carrier with the Old Globe Shakespeare Company. There were great actors there that summer: Victor Buono, Tim Matheson, John Glover, and Penny Fuller. Repertory included *Romeo and Juliet,* and *Henry IV, Part I.* I was doing the musical version of

Twelfth Night next door, playing the same role as Penny Fuller for three months. Everything was going great until one incident halfway through the season.

During a Saturday matinee, I got a message from stage management saying that Eric was trying to get a hold of me. We were having an understudy rehearsal, so I was already at the theater. It was about an hour and a half before curtain. I called Eric at home, and he said he'd just gotten a call from my mother saying she wanted to come to the theater. "She sound really drunk, Robin. What should I do? I've gotta be there in a half hour."

I said, "Well, see if you can get over there and make sure she has something to eat. And if she's not too bad, bring her on over."

He said, "Well, okay, but I don't want to be late."

I said, "Thanks Eric. Thanks for doing this, and let me know what happens. If not, just leave her at the hotel."

He said, "Okay," and hung up.

A little while later, Eric came running backstage, holding part of his costume. He said, "Robin, your mom is out on the lawn. I tried to put her in a cab, but she just won't go. She's falling-down drunk."

"Why didn't you leave her at the hotel?" I blurted out.

"You told me to get her something to eat. I took her to McDonald's and got her a cheeseburger and a strawberry milkshake. As I started to drive her back, she spilled it all down the front of her dress. We were close to the theater, so I thought I'd bring her backstage to clean her off, but I couldn't get her through the stage door. She got away and started laughing and giggling on the lawn with the Renaissance dancers, and before I could get to her, she was laying out on her ass."

"Where is she now?" I said, over the fifteen-minute call to curtain.

Eric said, "Well, I had to sign in, and one of the apprentice costume kids went to get her some coffee. They're gonna try to get her in a cab and back to the Hilton."

Neither of us were in any position to leave the theater since both our curtains would go up at the same time, two o'clock. Eric left to get dressed, and I finished getting into costume. I was so upset and angry, I was shaking, and tears welled up in my eyes. I hoped she was in a cab and on her way out of there. I was an actress, and I had a show to do. It didn't matter that the audience was composed of blue-haired people and tourists who couldn't get into the zoo. I had a performance to give. I was a union actress. Despite my professionalism, I cried all the way through. Still, my stage manager thought it was the best performance I'd ever given.

I heard at intermission that the costume kids had called a cab, but because of the traffic going in and out of Balboa Park and the Hispanic Dance Concert happening at the Bowl, the cab couldn't get through. Edna, a costumer, had to sit on one of the benches with my mother out on the green. But she had to leave because she had a costume change coming up after the first scene. So my mother was left alone, which was not a good thing. She waddled over to the Old Globe's doors and began pounding on them with her fists. She yelled in a syrupy, Southern drawl, "Lemme in, lemme in! Robin Rae, open the door!" The volunteer ushers and acting interns had to forcibly eject my mother and peel her off the theater's front door. They held her there while one went to find the wandering cab. Thankfully, they got her out of there before intermission.

This event was the talk of the week. If Victor Buono hadn't been so kind and sympathetic, I'm sure my scars would have been deeper. But he had stories that even rivaled mine. My mother and stepfather never saw my performance.

33

Which One?

Spring 1980

Much to my surprise, the costume-fitting place was in a long trailer. I'd been hired to do a movie-of-the-week, and I expected a lot more from Universal Studios. I was to play the ugly duckling. It was a small part, about four days worth of work in total and I was being fitted for three different scenes. A tall thin man came into my fitting room, pulling aside the curtain and asked, "Are you Robin Taylor?"

Covering my bra with my hands, I said, "Yes, I am."

He said, "There's a telephone call for you."

"A telephone call for me? Here?"

Closing the curtain, he said, "Yes. It's in the supervisor's room."

I threw on an unbuttoned shirt and followed him down the long trailer corridor and into another room. Picking up the big black phone, I said, "Hello."

It was Eric on the other line. "Robin, your dad's had a stroke."

Astonished, I said, "My dad! Which one?"

"Tiny," he said.

"Tiny, my real dad?"

"Yes," he said. "I'm sorry. I just didn't think this phone call should wait."

"Where is he?" I asked with no emotion to my voice.

"He's in Seattle. I guess it happened at work," Eric said. "And they've moved him to the Swedish Hospital."

"Oh," I said, swallowing hard. It had been at least five years since I had spoken with him. "Call my friend Jane in Seattle," I continued, "and ask if she can send some flowers over to the hospital. Tell her I'll send her some money. Tell her to sign the card 'From Robin and Eric.'"

Eric sounded a bit flustered, but he said he'd do it. "Are you doing okay?" he asked.

"Yeah. This is weird, huh, Eric?"

"Yeah," he said. "Tiny having a stroke, and he's so young."

"I'd better get back to my fitting. Thanks for the call, Eric, and see if you can get through to Jane, okay?"

"All right," Eric said, "Love you."

"Love you too." I hung up the phone. I don't remember feeling anything; I just went about my business.

Exactly a week later, on Good Friday, March 7, I was out on location at Malibu Lake when I got called over by the second assistant director.

"Robin. Robin. Phone call for you. Here, take it on the portable. They say it's an emergency."

Luckily, we were only blocking for camera, and I was

in the back in the scene and had no lines. I stepped through the light setup and over the mound of fake snow to where the second assistant director held up the phone.

"Hello?" I said into the mouthpiece as it crackled and snapped.

"Robin, it's Eric. Sorry to bother you on the set."

"Yeah, Eric, what's up? What's wrong?" I said, my voice dropping. "Is Tiny dead?"

There was a pause, and then he said "No, it's not Tiny, it's Phil."

"Phil? Phil who?"

"Phil," Eric said. "Your stepfather. He's dead."

"What do you mean, Phil's dead?"

"He died of a massive coronary," he replied. "A stroke."

"You're kidding! What do you mean? How'd it happen?"

"It happened last night when your mom and he were moving into the new condo," Eric said. "When he went to bed, he had a massive coronary and died in his sleep."

Stunned and standing in ankle-deep mud, I was amazed at this coincidence. A week apart, two fathers, two strokes."

Years before I would get messages from my answering service saying. "Your father called to say he's in town." I would ask, "Which one?"

The answering service operator would reply, "What?"

"Well, which father?"

And she'd say with laughter in her voice, "Well, I don't know."

171

"Okay, where are they staying?" If it was the Tropicana on Sunset Boulevard, I'd know it was Tiny. If it was the Plaza in Century City on the Avenue of the Stars, I'd know it was Phil.

34

Finished Business

Winter 1994

It had been ten years since I was discharged from the
psychiatric hospital. Late one Sunday, after working a
full day at my Grand Street art studio, I sat down to
eat from a pasteboard box of moo goo gai pan from the
Chinese takeout around the corner. Leisurely poking at
the food, I flipped through the *New York Times Sunday
Magazine*. A headline made me freeze. "Letting Go of
Payne Whitney: The Recent Demolition and Demise of
the Fabled Psychiatric Clinic." Although a decade had
passed, I clearly remembered my last look at the place.

It had been a drizzly and warm morning. I had a
one-way bus ticket to Kansas City, Missouri, in my
zippered shoulder bag, and I wasn't looking back. Mark,
my constant friend all these years, had brought me a neatly
packed suitcase filled with lightweight clothes. He also
found the special object I asked for: The worn-out Mr.
Navy that Tiny gave me when I was almost two.

Eric was expecting me on January 1 on a Delta flight

from Kansas City to Burbank. So I had to make that 2 p.m. Greyhound bus.

Stepping out of the hospital driveway onto First Avenue, I hailed a taxi. As we headed west toward Central Park, I asked the driver if he would please go down Fifth Avenue to Port Authority. It was nearing New Year's Eve, and I wanted to see the leftover Christmas decorations before I left the city. The last holiday I could recall was Easter.

I made the two o'clock out of the Port Authority bus terminal and before I knew it, I was looking back at Manhattan from the New Jersey side of the tunnel. There was something I had to do in Missouri and that was the only clear thing I had on my mind.

People came and went on the bus, but I couldn't describe who or how many. The next day, just before we reached St. Louis, the snow started to fall. When we crossed the brown Mississippi and drove into the city, the hairs on my back of my spine started to prick up. Pictures and memories began to snowball on top of each other. I could smell them, taste them, I could feel the August heat speeding by Tallulah's open window. It projected me back into the Missouri nightmare where I'd been left by the side of the road.

Wiping the condensation off the window with my sleeve, I watched us pull out of the St. Louis bus station. The rolling countryside of eastern Missouri changed into long winding stretches of Ozark plains. The white highway led us by roadside fences lightly sung to by whispering snow.

The bus downshifted, jerked back, and pulled off onto

a rising off-ramp. We were heading toward a restaurant and large gas stop area. The mood of the passengers changed. They licked their lips and muttered about hot chocolate, coffee, and cellophane sandwiches. I felt strangely alert.

"Fifteen minutes," the driver said and, slapping his hands together, went off toward the restaurant door.

I brought down the small suitcase above my head, opened it and pulled out my dirty one-armed old Mr. Navy. I returned the suitcase to its place and stepped out of the bus.

Snow fell heavily. Everyone was in the fogged-glass-covered diner. Behind the restaurant and empty parking lot there was an open field. There was a rise on a hill and the remains of what looked like an old farmer's shack.

Crunching my way over to the wooden shack, I carefully but very diligently began to dig a hole with my pocket pen. The more I dug, the angrier I became until somehow I lost the pen and started digging with my fingers. Taking the sock doll out of my right pocket, I laid it with its back against the rotting wood. Mr. Navy looked back at me with its button eyes. My warm tears melted the snow around where they fell. Soon great sobs engulfed me as I shoved the snow back up against the doll, burying it under a mound of crusted white.

Standing up with wet knees and feet I turned and walked back toward the parking lot. Before I stepped onto the pavement, I turned and looked back at the wooden shack. That's where it belonged, back at the beginning. I didn't want the doll anymore. I didn't want the memories. I had to let go.

A great feeling of sadness washed over me. Yet at the

same time, I felt light, so light I don't even remember walking back to the bus. When I climbed aboard, the bus was almost full again. I saw happy people holding steaming coffee in paper cups. Some of the children were sipping foaming hot chocolate, but that was okay, I didn't mind.

I sat back down in my seat without undoing my coat; I wiped the frosted pane of glass and peered out. I could see the small rise of the hill, and the rotted shack leaning against the snowy mound. Gusts of wind obscured my view as the bus jerked and headed out. I could see it more clearly once we got on the highway. It was the first time I felt a clear emptiness. It was a pure innocence of self, a thirst to know more.

My past was done. I still did not know who I was, but now I could rebuild. I could stand on top of all my memories and step toward a future. I would find that voice. I would speak and live my own truth. The whole world was now open for me and the truth about Robin.